D0775849

Besides being beautiful little hand-sized objects
themselves, showcasing exceptional writing, the
wonder of these books is that they exist at all . . .
Uniformly excellent, engaging, thought-provoking,
and informative."

Jennifer Bort Yacovissi, *Washington Independent
Review of Books*

. . . edifying and entertaining . . . perfect for slipping
in a pocket and pulling out when life is on hold."

Sarah Murdoch, *Toronto Star*

For my money, Object Lessons is the most consistently
interesting nonfiction book series in America."

Megan Volpert, *PopMatters*

Though short, at roughly 25,000 words apiece, these
books are anything but slight."

Marina Benjamin, *New Statesman*

[W]itty, thought-provoking, and poetic . . . These little
books are a page-flipper's dream."

John Timpane, *The Philadelphia Inquirer*

OBJECT LESSONS

A book series about the hidden lives of ordinary things.

Series Editors:

Ian Bogost and Christopher Schaberg

Advisory Board:

Sara Ahmed, Jane Bennett, Jeffrey Jerome Cohen, Johanna Drucker, Raiford Guins, Graham Harman, renée hoogland, Pam Houston, Eileen Joy, Douglas Kahn, Daniel Miller, Esther Milne, Timothy Morton, Kathleen Stewart, Nigel Thrift, Rob Walker, Michele White.

In association with

Narrative Storytelling Initiative

BOOKS IN THE SERIES

hyphen

PARDIS MAHDAVI

BLOOMSBURY ACADEMIC
NEW YORK • LONDON • OXFORD • NEW DELHI • SYDNEY

BLOOMSBURY ACADEMIC
Bloomsbury Publishing Inc
1385 Broadway, New York, NY 10018, USA
50 Bedford Square, London, WC1B 3DP, UK
29 Earlsfort Terrace, Dublin 2, Ireland

BLOOMSBURY, BLOOMSBURY ACADEMIC and the Diana logo are
trademarks of Bloomsbury Publishing Plc

First published in the United States of America 2021

ISBN: PB: 978-1-5013-7390-9
ePDF: 978-1-5013-7392-3
eBook: 978-1-5013-7391-6

Series: Object Lessons

Typeset by Deanta Global Publishing Services, Chennai, India
Printed and bound in the United States of America

To find out more about our authors and books visit www.bloomsbury.com
and sign up for our newsletters.

For Shayan, who asked the question

CONTENTS

PART 2 HYPHEN AS DIVIDER

PART 3 THE DEATH AND RE-BIRTH OF THE HYPHEN(ATED)

AUTHOR'S NOTE

To protect confidentiality, all names and identifying information have been changed throughout the text except when I refer to myself or my own family.

PREFACE

To hyphenate or not to hyphenate has been a central point of controversy since before the imprinting of the first Gutenberg Bible. And yet, the hyphen has persisted, bringing and bridging new words and concepts. The journey of this humble piece of connective punctuation reveals the quiet power of an orthographic concept to speak to the travails of hyphenated individuals all over the world.

It took being kicked out of my ancestral home to wrap my limbs around the hyphen. As a hyphenated Iranian-American growing up betwixt and between, I have struggled to find or make belonging. And I have learned that I am not alone. Like many others whom I introduce in this book, I have learned that I don't have to fit on one side of the hyphen or the other—but rather I can embrace the space between. So many others like me have finally found a way to embrace their voice and the authority inside the hyphen itself.

I invite you to join us to see how the journey of a humble grammatical marker has the potential to make belonging for hyphenated individuals struggling through identity politics today.

PART 1

ANCESTORS WORSHIPPED

1 MY BIG FAT PERSIAN WEDDING

Every time I said my name in school, I felt caught between two worlds. Should I say my name as it was written in Persian with equal weight between the two syllables *Par* and *dis* as my parents did? Or should I make things easier for my American teachers and classmates who wanted to Anglicize my name by focusing either on the last syllable—saying Par-*dis* or just muttering the ugly *Prds*—erasing the vowels from my name altogether? When I tried to correct people, their non-native Persian-speaking brains could not comprehend my pronunciation, and so it came that I began introducing myself with the Anglicized version of my name, feeling a little pinch each time I did so.

My family left Iran in 1978 due to the impending Iranian Revolution. But, instead of moving to a big city with other migrants and refugees, my parents decided to settle in a suburb outside Minneapolis where we were among the only Brown people the community had ever seen. Rather than try to integrate or assimilate, my parents held fiercely to their Iranian-ness, insisting on speaking Persian loudly in public, and outfitting me in traditional Iranian dress instead of allowing me to venture into denim.

The spring and summer of 1985 stand out in my mind as heightened months of liminality.

It was an unusually warm spring day for Minneapolis, and my backpack's right strap dug into my shoulder as I swung it around to my front so I could hunt for the small Ziploc baggie of breadcrumbs I had stashed before school. My plan was to convince my mother to let me feed the duck family living on the lake near our house. That's when I knocked into my four-year-old brother, Paymohn, and he screamed loud enough for my mother to turn around from the front seat of our Volvo. She started yelling at me in rapid Persian.

"What are you doing? Do I need to pull over? Apologize to your brother right now! You are the older sister, set a better example."

"Only three years older," I muttered under my breath as I slunk deeper into the folds of the cream-colored, leather-lined seats. I looked out the window to be sure no one had heard my mother screaming—not because I was embarrassed about being yelled at, but because I was worried people would hear her speaking in what Minnesotans commonly referred to as "that funny language."

I was only seven years old in 1985, but I knew the importance of appearance and language. My attempts at coming off as the quintessential American seven-year-old were thwarted regularly by my maternal grandmother who lived with us in Wayazata. My grandmother refused to learn English and insisted on packing my lunchbox full of Persian rice and stews made with aromatic spices like coriander and fenugreek leaves that wafted throughout the cafeteria.

And if my name wasn't bad enough, the thick black hair that seemed to grow out of every pore on my body was an additional marker of my otherness. The kids at Woods Academy teased me so badly that on many days I wanted to stay at home in the comfort of my grandmother's lap.

On this particular morning, I had begged my parents to let me stay home from school. "The kids have gotten meaner somehow," I said in English. My mother flashed me *the look*, demanding that I switch back to Persian. I was stubborn in my desire to acculturate and refused; only if I caught my grandmother's sad eyes would I acquiesce, not wanting her to be left out.

My father bounded down the stairs with my brother clinging to his leg. One hand cradled my brother's head in his hands while the other was buttoning his over-starched white oxford shirt. My mother quickly told him that I wanted to stay home from school.

"School is your job," my father said. He then launched into his usual lecture about the importance of education.

"They can take everything from you, Pardis. They can take your home, your belongings," my father lectured, "they can even take your country. But the one thing that no one can ever take from you is your education. They can never take your mind."

My father's whole life revolved around his education. My parents had met in Iran in the early 1970s before my father came to the United States in 1972 as a chief resident at the University of Chicago Medical Center. Americans were eager for well-trained Iranian physicians, and my father, like my two uncles, had been recruited straight from Tehran University Medical School after he completed his residency and mandatory military service of two years.

My father had met my mother only briefly in Iran through her brother who was, at the time, my father's roommate. My mother, who attended a French Catholic school in Tehran most of her life, had been accepted to University of Montreal for her bachelor's degree. Her father had recently died, and she and my grandmother decided to try living abroad for a few years; Canada made sense to them because they both spoke French, but not English. When my uncle and father were sent to Chicago, my mother and grandmother decided to pay them a visit on their way to Montreal.

My mother never made it to Montreal. What was supposed to have been a two week stop-over in Chicago to help my uncle settle in turned into a four-year relationship with my father that ended with them returning to Tehran to marry and start a family. My mother un-enrolled from the University of Montreal, and learned English by tutoring my uncle's girlfriends in Persian in exchange for English tutoring. She also enrolled at the University of Illinois, Chicago, where she studied industrial engineering.

A few weeks after she graduated, she and my father returned to Tehran for what appeared—from the faded photographs on our walls—to have been a spectacular wedding. My mother was thrilled to be home in Tehran. But this was 1977, and her joy was short-lived as the revolution was already brewing.

My parents were against the shah and marched in the streets, calling for his removal. People were being arrested following the protests, and my father began to realize that it was going to be dangerous for them to stay in their native country. It was he who initially begged my mother to leave Iran and return to the United States. At the time, he could still return to his job in Chicago. My mother (who would pass on her stubbornness to me) refused. There was nothing in Chicago for her, she told him. And they owed it to their country to stay.

Six months later my mother was arrested after marching in a protest. When she was released, she realized she was pregnant. My father was thrilled by this news, but it also made him even more determined to convince my mother to leave. He was certain that Iran was not a safe place to raise a family. By now, his position in Chicago was no longer available, but that did not weaken his resolve. He searched and found a job in Minneapolis and went ahead of my mother to find a house and a graduate program where she could pursue her studies.

In July 1978, my father called Tehran and told my mother she had been admitted with a full scholarship. Belly swollen, nationalism deflated, my mother agreed to join him in

Minnesota on one condition—my grandmother would come along as well. My father agreed. In August, my mother was eight months pregnant with me, and she boarded the last plane that left Tehran to the United States for the next forty years. It was also the last international flight to depart for some months while the revolution bubbled through the country.

This was a story my parents told me weekly. It was the story of their sacrifice: of how they lost everything in Iran but were able to survive in America because of—and through their—education. Education was the only global currency that could keep you alive, and it was my job to keep earning mine.

So, on that spring day in 1985, I pulled on my red and blue outercoat and slung my backpack over my shoulder, getting ready to trudge to school. My grandmother sensed my buzzing irritation and slowly came to the door where my mother was kneeling to help me tie my shoelaces.

"I think the mother duck finally had her ducklings," she whispered in my ear.

I watched her place the Ziploc bag filled with breadcrumbs in my backpack. My mother looked up to see what her mother was doing.

"Maybe stop by to see the ducks today after school," my grandmother instructed my mother. My mother nodded silently and instantly I felt better.

That day at school things were surprisingly calm. No one teased me about my fragrant lunch, and during P.E. I wasn't even the last one picked for the dodgeball teams. By the afternoon, I was actually glad I had come to school.

I spotted my mother's blue Volvo and jumped into the car. I then pulled out the baggie of breadcrumbs, figuring that if I could get my brother excited about the ducks, we would be certain to have longer at the lake. Paymohn grabbed the baggie out of my hand and started shaking it.

My mother turned around again, her olive skin flushed red. "What are you doing with that?! You are going to make a mess!" My mother grabbed the breadcrumbs and stuffed them into the car's ashtray.

I felt hot tears spring to my eyes because I knew this meant we weren't going to stop at the lake after all.

"It's okay, Dabis," Paymohn said, using the version of my name that his three-year-old tongue could manage to produce. "Ghamarjoon will walk us there later, after Mommy goes back to work," he added, referring to our grandmother.

Our mother had to return to my father's medical practice where she was in charge of billing and practice management. She had finished her master's in international communication but never had a chance to use it. Instead of pursuing her own dreams, she swam into the medical field to help her husband. Before long she was pregnant with my brother, and her hopes of becoming a journalist drifted further away, never to return.

It wasn't until many years later, when I had three children of my own and was trying to run a school, that I understood the depth of her fatigue. The exhaustion of her work–life balance was exacerbated by the precarity of our position as

Iranians their in the United States. She and my father had completed education here, and both of her children were American born, but she still kept a suitcase packed in the corner of the house, always ready for departure, to return home.

The weight of uncertainty—of not knowing if, or when, she may return home—was yet another thing my mother carried around in that enormous sack on her shoulders. She carried her children, mother, husband, brothers, and her home country around with her at all times. No wonder she was so tired.

I caught my mother's eyes in the rear-view mirror and noticed the purple circles that had deepened there. My tears retreated, and I felt a wince of pity for my mom. As we pulled up to the house, she asked if we could get out and walk to the front door so that she didn't have to pull into the garage.

She was running late again. I agreed and pulled first my backpack, and then my brother out of the car. As the Volvo crept away, my brother and I slowly walked up to the front door hand in hand. We were careful not to step on the cracks in the pavement—a game we loved to play, where we pretended they contained molten lava. In the summers, when moss grew between the cracks, we felt vindicated in our imaginations.

As we hopped closer to the brown wood carved door, I noticed that a large sign had been taped to the door. Red letters sprawled across a white backdrop, and an American flag was drawn at the bottom. My brother couldn't read, but he squeezed my hand in fear. He knew enough to sense that the sign was not friendly.

We walked up closer and I could see each angry letter, spelling out the message of hate.

"BURN THIS HOUSE, TERRORISTS LIVE HERE"

I read it out loud to my brother, my voice shaking.

"What does it mean?" he asked, his lips trembling.

My fear quickly turned to anger, and I started kicking the door. I went to pull the sign down, but the door swung open before I had the chance, and I fell forward into my grandmother's arms.

Ghamarjoon asked us what had happened. I pulled out of the hug and took her hand to show her the sign. She couldn't read English, so I read it aloud again, bile coming into my mouth as I spoke the vile words.

She stood silently looking it. It dawned on me that even though she didn't understand the words, she could feel the wickedness just as my brother had. I translated it for her. Before I could even finish, she was running to the phone on our kitchen wall.

I dropped my backpack, which felt heavier somehow. Paymohn slammed the door shut, willing the words to stay outside and not penetrate in. I heard my grandmother talking to my father, ordering her son-in-law to come home at once.

I grabbed my brother's arm and ran downstairs to the basement. As we descended, I heard the television. My grandmother watched Iranian satellite TV all day long—an umbilical cord to the home country that she would never cut, even after forty years of living in the United States. The announcer was speaking in rapid, formal Persian that I strained to understand with my "kitchen Farsi." As my brother and I drew closer, we saw the face of Ayatollah Khomeini standing over a crowd that was burning American flags in celebration.

The camera panned to what was once the US Embassy in Tehran, which Khomeini had re-labeled the "Den of Spies."[1] Angry people were spray-painting graffiti on the walls. My stomach sank. I looked over at Paymohn who was silently watching. The effects of this day would live within us for the rest of our lives.

That evening when my father came home from work, the house was unusually silent. From our play area in the basement, Paymohn and I heard whispers upstairs and the sound of padded feet pacing the kitchen. When we came up for dinner, my father sat us down and looked at us deeply, in that way he had of piercing our souls with his eyes.

"We are moving to California. It's not safe here for us anymore," my father announced.

Paymohn and I both nodded, too afraid to say anything or ask any questions. The next day my father flew to California on a scouting trip.

While he was away, Paymohn and I stayed home from school, watching the television for clues as to what was happening. On the Iranian satellite channels, we saw Iran decrying our home country, the United States, as "the Great Satan." On the English channels, we heard American officials denounce Iran as the "greatest threat to the American way of life and values." And our confusion grew deeper. If Iran were pitted against America, what were we to think about the two of us who were Iran and America at once?

One month later, we moved to southern California, and I spent the rest of my formative years in the safety of a place where more than one million Iranians live. For college, I stayed in southern California, afraid to venture out into the unknown. Still, growing up with hundreds of thousands of other Iranian-Americans didn't help my identity crisis. If anything, I grew more and more confused.

My mother remained firm that in our home, we would carry out "Iranian values"—as defined by her. That meant no sleep overs, no boyfriends, no makeup. If I did something she didn't like, my mother chastised me for becoming too American; but at school, I was too Iranian, always other. And so, in college, I chose to study diplomacy, in an attempt to bridge the two sides of me that raged a growing war across continents. It wasn't until I began studying activism, social movements, feminist theory, and identity politics that I began to find my feet.

Does a hyphen connect or divide? This has been a central controversy surrounding the important orthographic concept of the hyphen. Even as we focus on whether to hyphenate two words or not, we have forgotten the history, the journey, and the power of the hyphen itself. "Hyphen" is derived from an ancient Greek word meaning "to tie together." Indeed, the origin of the hyphen dates back to the ancient Greek grammarian, Dionysis Thrax,[2] deploying this grammatical mark to denote the connection, the bringing together, of words before spaces between words became common.

This book explores how four hyphenated individuals who feel marginalized in society make belonging by finding power in the hyphen itself. Our journey mirrors the journey of this orthographic concept, moving between foci on the words that the hyphen brings together, to focusing on the authority within the hyphen itself. Through self-exploration, we look at the intersections of identity politics, sexual politics, and the politics of belonging. In addition to my story, we meet three other individuals who are each on a similar journey. We watch as they find a way to embrace the space of the hyphen—rejecting the false choice of trying to fit into previously prescribed identities—and map their journey through the public sphere. Through their stories, we collectively consider how making belonging as hyphenated Americans serves to fulfill the failures of troubled states, regimes, or institutions, and offer possibilities to navigate, articulate, and empower new identities.

2 U-HYPHENS

Dionysus Thrax, the tax-evading, second-century Greek grammarian, gave birth to the hyphen when he was caught between two worlds. Should he be spending his time adding to punctuation rules that his teacher Aristarchus—he of asterisk fame—asked him to refine? Or, should he give in to his heart's desire to focus on the spoken word? As he roamed the halls of the Library of Alexandria, he realized that he could do both. And so, the hyphen was born.[1]

As Thrax looked at the words that filled the expensive parchment paper surrounding him, he was concerned. There were no spaces. How would a reader—or a singer, as readers often preferred to sing the text—know where to put emphasis on certain words? What words *belonged* together? What words needed to be joined?

Thrax set to work on an essay entitled "*Tekhne Grammatike*" or "The Art of Grammar." In this piece he focused on the state of the art of grammar, exploring the construction of words and introducing possibilities for new construction. Thrax drew inspiration from his teacher, Aristarchus, as well as Aristarchus' mentor, Aristophanes, who was known as the father of Greek punctuation. "*Tekhne*" became an instant success, and the scribal practices that Thrax suggested would be adopted and employed by Greek scribes for centuries to come.

In the opening section of the essay, Thrax focused on prosody, or the spoken delivery of written text. He introduced new punctuation that would facilitate the delivery, rhythms, and intonation of the written word for speakers and singers alike. After introducing the *apostrophe* to clarify syllable boundaries that were ambiguous, and the comma-like *hypodiastole* that would separate concepts, Thrax gave us the *hyphen,* a U-like construction placed under adjacent words that clarified for the speaker that the words should be understood—and spoken—as a single entity. The *hyphen*, the *apostrophe* and the *hypodiastole* became vital components of writing and speaking to bring clarity for the reader and speaker in interpreting the author's intent.

Thrax's hyphen—which would later be re-named a "sublinear hyphen" because it was used as a small bow shape written beneath two words—remained in popular use in Greek texts for centuries. But, like many other casualties of empire, the Greeks would see their beloved hyphen robbed, ransacked, and reformed by the brutal Romans some three hundred years later.

Like many other unfortunate social transformations, it was a combination of colonialism and capitalism that took the hyphen from a magical marker to show belonging in word construction, to a facilitator for eighth century non-native speaking scribes who did not want to procure new parchment paper when they made mistakes in order to keep costs of texts low. While the Romans had initially adopted the Greek writing practice of writing without spaces (causing them to remove the dots they had previously used to separate words), by the eighth century, Celtic monks who were struggling with the unspaced Latin texts found a new use for the hyphen that the Romans would quickly adopt. The Celtic scribes struggled to pry apart smashed-together words and concepts that their non-Latin speaking linguistic skills could not grasp. In turn, they broke up and inserted words in error, dividing texts in an attempt to make sense of them. In this process, they made mistakes.

But rather than start their writing over or procuring a new piece of stone or parchment, they decided to make a new purpose for the hyphen—to divide and conquer. They used the hyphen to divide words or concepts they did not understand, and to cover up their errors. The scribes found it was easier to use their razors to erase and then cover up with a straight line placed in the middle. And thus, the elegant, sublinear bow-shaped U-hyphen that was used to fuse words and highlight words that belonged together was erased and replaced with a straight-line dividing marker of punctuation.

This would be codified in the Gutenberg Bible centuries later, much to the chagrin of the Greeks, who felt an important part of their past erased by what they considered to be a hostile takeover of a previously loved grammatical mark.

Some two thousand years later when Toula Portokalos' father Gus in the popular film *My Big Fat Greek Wedding* would claim that everything was invented by the Greeks, hyphenophiles who knew the real story of their orthographic marker would sigh in agreement, mourning for Dionysus Thrax and his dreams for the hyphen.[2]

3 ANCESTORS HEAR MY PRAYERS

Daniel's heart started pounding when he heard the familiar ping announcing the arrival of a text message. He sat straight up in bed, fumbling around for his glasses. He squinted at the glowing blue of his bedside clock. 10 a.m. He had slept in again. His mother would be waiting in the kitchen, ready for a lecture about discipline, or Daniel's lack thereof.

Glasses on, he reached for his phone, hungry with anticipation. He felt the entirety of his seventeen-year-old body tremble when he saw the sender's name: Ronnie.

"CUM OVER. NOW"

A command. One that Daniel had been waiting for since his friend Jason had introduced him to Ronnie at a concert weeks ago. Ronnie was exactly Daniel's type: tall, muscular, thick curling black hair, and dark brown—almost black— eyes that seemed to devour Daniel as the two of them shared drinks. Jason had described Ronnie as a "Rice Queen"—a non-Asian-American man who was attracted almost exclusively to Asian and Asian-American men. Since that night, Daniel and Ronnie had been exchanging text messages every few days.

Daniel swung his legs out of bed and sighed as his bare feet touched the cool floor of his bedroom. He smiled as the feather light touch of his fingers turned on his phallic cylindrical lamp, illuminating his small bedroom in a glowing gold light. He shuffled toward the window and leaned his head against the glass as he looked down.

A city that never sleeps, Daniel reminded himself as he watched the cars pile up on Broadway. In two months, he would leave New York City—his home since birth—and travel to California to begin his college career at a small liberal arts college outside of Los Angeles. New York had defined his parents after they left Shanghai, and for a long time, it had defined him too. He took his cues on how to dress, how to cut an edge in his voice, and how to move through space from other New Yorkers. The City, as New Yorkers referred to their hometown, was filled with gay men, so Daniel never had any anxiety about coming out. But as hard as he tried, he could never completely fit in with the "gay scene" in the City. He didn't have the same appetite for working out that many of his counter parts did; and while he enjoyed the abundance of clubs, raves, and parties within a two mile radius of his apartment, he found that he preferred one-on-on meals, quiet evenings in hole-in-the-wall cafes, or just chatting on his computer as he sat curled up in the bed he had outgrown years ago.

Daniel opened the window and felt his thin black hair curl as the humidity sank in. He quickly pulled his head back inside and began smoothing his cowlick with his hand. He crept quietly into the bathroom—taking care to avoid his mother who was clearly making *xiao long bao* (soup dumplings)—and slipped his contacts in after taking a quick rinse in the shower, washing off the sleep and sweat that had started to overtake him in bed. He threw on his favorite tight jeans and a crewneck sweater and dug out his worn adidas sneakers. He inhaled the familiarly intoxicating scent of his mother's cooking—soup dumplings were his favorite.

A burst of color and a rainbow of smells awaited Daniel in the kitchen. His mother had laid out rows and rows of washed green vegetables which complemented the reds, yellows, and whites of the pastries she had stayed up all night making.

"Lazy," his mother barked, followed by more mutterings in Mandarin. Daniel had briefly considered learning his native tongue but decided against it when his father insisted it wasn't necessary. Still, he had picked up some from all the time he spent with his mother and her friends in Chinatown over the years. Daniel shook his head and curled his lithe body around his mother to sneak a pork *bao*. His mother slapped his hand but not before he had a chance to pop the delicious treat into his mouth.

Just then his mother looked down at her son's shoes. "Why are you wearing shoes indoors?" she demanded. "And wait, were you planning on *going somewhere?*"

Daniel's eyes floated across the elaborate meal preparations over to the altars on the side of the living room. He
clicked on his phone, and indeed it was July 15th. All of July
was Ghost Month—a time when Taoists and Buddhists like
his family believed that the ghosts of ancestors roamed the
earth. July 15th was *Zhong Yuan Jie,* the Hungry Ghosts Festival.[1] Offerings had to be prepared to soothe the spirits of the
ancestors. More than the Mooncake festival or Chinese New
Year, Daniel's mother threw herself into preparations for the
Ghost Festival. And usually Daniel, ever the dutiful Chinese-
American son, helped her every step of the way.

Daniel's phone pinged again.

"CUMING?"

He felt beads of sweat forming; he was desperate to see
Ronnie. But his mother's face warned that this was not going
to be easy.

"I'm going out," Daniel announced.

"Excuse me?" his mother responded. "First you sleep in,
lazy, disgusting. Now you are walking out on me? On *Zhong
Yuan Jie?!*"

Daniel froze for a moment. He felt his phone buzzing in his
pocket. He looked at his mother's angry face. He remembered
the ghost money he was supposed to offer to the ancestors.
Torn, again. He grabbed a MetroCard, shoved it in his back
pocket and ran out the door. He could hear his mother's
yells—a mix of Mandarin and English—as he tried not to
tumble down the three flights of stairs of their Chinatown
walk-up. He headed toward the 1-9 red line subway that

would take him all the way uptown. In New York City terms, Daniel and Ronnie lived on opposite ends of the world. Daniel lived in a small one-bedroom apartment downtown that his parents had converted into a "two-bedroom" by erecting a wall at the corner of the living room to produce a bedroom for Daniel. Ronnie lived in Washington Heights, just north of Harlem.

While onboard the train, Daniel felt his stomach sink. He kept hearing his mother's voice in his head and could almost feel the ancestor ghosts following him, shaming him for not keeping their culture alive. But he was so certain from the weeks of texting with Ronnie, that the two had a real connection—one that Daniel could see turning into love. He felt Ronnie understood him in ways that other partners had not. When Daniel emerged from the subway it was pouring rain. The sheets of water crashed down on him and bounced back up from the sidewalk as he curled himself under his now soaked denim jacket. It was a twenty minute walk from the metro stop to Ronnie's apartment. When Daniel arrived, he felt like a drowned rat.

Ronnie buzzed him in, and Daniel fought a shiver as he climbed the stairs. The air conditioning froze his wet skin to the bone, but he tried to shake it off. Daniel wondered if the ancestors had made it rain to teach him a lesson. He suddenly wished he were a ghost and could float between worlds seamlessly. He felt acutely uncomfortable in his own skin—unsure of what to make of his limbs, his skin color, and his various genitalia.

As he walked into Ronnie's apartment and began drying off, his phone buzzed again and again.

"THE GHOSTS WILL FIND YOU TODAY." It was his mother.

"HOW DARE YOU LEAVE ON GHOST FESTIVAL?!!! AIIYAH!" His grandmother.

"DISRESPECTFUL SON. THIS IS WHAT AMERICA DOES TO GOOD BOYS?" His auntie *Nya Nya*, texting from Shanghai.

And the texts kept coming. Daniel wanted to focus on Ronnie, but the phone weighed heavy in his pocket. At one point when Daniel and Ronnie were kissing, he could swear he saw a ghost. Ronnie pulled back.

"You seem distracted, sweet. What's up?" Ronnie asked. Daniel shook his head.

"It's Ghost Festival today," Daniel whispered. And suddenly he felt a wave of tears come crashing over him. Before he knew it, he was sobbing into Ronnie's pillow.

"Get dressed," Ronnie commanded. "We're going back to your ma's and we're gonna worship the shit out of your ancestors."

Daniel was too broken to protest. He let Ronnie lend him some clothes which were four sizes too big (Daniel's were still soaking wet), but Daniel didn't care. He zipped up the FUBU hoodie, pulled on his wet adidas and followed his new beau back to the subway.

After a long, quiet ride, the two arrived back in Chinatown and silently entered the apartment.

Daniel's mother was sitting at the altar, bathed in incense. Her eyes were closed, but Daniel could see the tears streaming down her face. She opened them when she heard the front door shut.

She rubbed her eyes as she looked from her son—what was he wearing?—to the tall Black man standing next to Daniel. Ronnie squeezed Daniel's hand and his mother screamed.

A torrent of Mandarin words flew out of his mother's mouth, and while Daniel could intuit what she was saying, he couldn't catch the details, exactly. At that moment, Daniel felt fully inside his five senses: he smelled the incense and aromas of dumplings simmering on the stove, he heard his mother's voice moving up and down octaves, he saw the lanterns falling from the ceiling, he tasted the beads of sweat sliding into his mouth, and then he felt Ronnie's hand squeezing his.

"Ronnie, you need to leave. Right now." Daniel said in a low voice. Ronnie looked at him, puzzled, but Daniel pushed him out the door.

His mother continued to alternate between wailing and screaming. She looked at the altars and begged the ancestors for mercy.

"What ghost has possessed my child?" she screamed. The pots on the stove were simmering over and Daniel ran to the kitchen to turn down the heat. When he re-appeared, his mother was standing very still in the living room. She fixed her icy gaze on her son.

"Who *was* that?" she asked. Daniel stood breathless and motionless. He had never come out to his mother, but always assumed she knew.

"That, that was Ronnie," Daniel managed to exhale. "He's my, um, he's my—"

But before he could answer, his mother cut him off. He would remember this moment as the erecting of a large wall between the two of them. "Ask not what you do not wish to know," he could hear his father saying when his mother had accused him of having 'illicit sex'. He left them two months later.

"Never mind that question. I don't care about him," his mother snapped. "The question I really have is who are *you?*"

The question hung in the air.

"Well, who are you?" she continued, narrowing her piercing black eyes. "You are not my child. You are a disgrace to the ancestors who we are supposed to be honoring. You dishonor the ancestors, you dishonor yourself. Our culture is all we have, and you have disgraced it. You are not a man. You are not Chinese. You are a ghost, that is all."

Daniel fell to his knees. He looked up to watch a red lantern fall.

4 HYPHEN JUSTIFICATION— GUTENBERG AND HIS TRAVAILS

For much of the 1440s Johannes Gutenberg—née Gensfleich—felt caught between two worlds. He was constantly traveling back and forth between his hometown of Mainsz, in the Rhine-Main area of Germany, and Strasbourg. The son of Friele Gensfleich, a goldsmith, Johannes knew that continuing the trade was his duty. And while he loved working with metals, his secret passion was writing and experimenting with prints.[1]

Caught between a sense of familial obligation, and a strong desire to strike out on his own, Johannes often felt torn. In the late 1420s, desperate to demonstrate his independence and creativity, Johannes declared that he was changing his inherited last name. Though he had been born Johannes Gensfleich—John Gooseflesh in translation—he announced that he would be henceforth known as Johannes Gutenberg—a name that roughly translated to beautiful mountain. He felt this name change lift a great weight from his shoulders, and gave himself permission to leave Mainsz for Strasbourg in a quest to forge his own identity.

But his independence was short-lived. His father quickly followed him to Strasbourg and publicly changed his name to Gutenberg to match. Worse still, his father learned that Johannes had been dabbling in poetry while at university in Strasbourg and was not happy. Before long, Johannes found himself being dragged back to Mainsz, and back to the goldsmithing that he was bound to. Johannes quickly felt his life spinning out of his control. And while he stayed up nights writing poetry, he was acutely aware that his every move was being watched by his parents.

For four years Johannes led what he would think of as a double life. Goldsmith by day, poet by night. And all the while, his head would spin with thoughts of a different way to write and document written texts. This challenging sense of liminality came to a head when his parents introduced him to a young woman from Strasbourg, Ennelin. He was told that they would be married by summer's end.

Watching his independence and entrepreneurial spirit slip through his fingers, Johannes decided on the morning of their wedding to escape Mainsz once again for Strasbourg, jilting Ennelin, and enraging his father.

This time, Johannes would find temporary shelter in a parish in Strasbourg. Living at the parish awakened a spiritual side that Johannes did not know lived inside of him. He began spending his days following the pastors around, transcribing verses of the Bible as they tumbled out of his mentors' mouths. Johannes continued to work on what he referred to as a "secret invention" in the evenings, dabbling in blocks that would ultimately come together as the basis for movable type. It was during this time that he also learned the importance of forgiveness and began the self-reflective journey of finding his way back to his family.

In 1451 Johannes's worlds began converging. His pastor told him about a popular cardinal, Nicholas of Kues—Cusanus was his Latin name—who had a reputation as something of a Renaissance man. Cusanus was interested in philosophy, in science, and in inventing. But he was most well-known for his fierce desire to reorganize the Catholic Church. Inspired by philosophical writings on the importance of unity, Cusanus had begun dedicating his life to a particular missive: the campaign to standardize the Church's daily manual: the Bible.

When Johannes learned that Cusanus was traveling to Mainsz, he saw an opportunity. He packed his bags, made his way back home, and, slowly, reconnected with his family. He waited for several weeks until one day Cusanus finally arrived.

Johannes listened carefully as the Cardinal made the convincing case for a unifying text or "missal." And in that moment, it all fell into place. The "secret invention" that Johannes had been working on for over a decade—the printing press—could be used for the one text that would be guaranteed to be an instant bestseller. Overflowing with excitement, Johannes returned home to share his idea with his father who, predictably, threw water on the flames of his son's passion. Johannes's father, Friele, favored a different version of the missal—the one put forward by the Archbishop of Mainsz. Friele chastised his son for being a traitor to his hometown and community by falling under the seductive spell of Cardinal Cusanus.

But Johannes knew that with no authorized, standardized version of the Bible on the horizon, and with Cusanus' increasing fame and repute, that the production of Cusanus' unifying Bible would be a hit. And so it was that Johannes moved out of his parents' home and into a small workshop that he purchased using the money he had saved up from selling polished metal mirrors for sale to pilgrims traveling to Aachen to visit the relics displayed by Emperor Charlemagne.

He got to work setting entire pages in pre-cast metal letters that could be impressed quickly and consistently. The result was a perfect 42-line Bible printed in a gorgeous densely spaced black-letter script. But perhaps the most astonishing quality of Gutenberg's 42-line Bible was the perfect uniformity of the text. Each line was elegantly justified, inspiring typographers for centuries to come. How did he get his text so perfectly justified? How did he avoid the usual wide-open spaces between words?

Gutenberg had an arsenal of techniques at his disposal. An artist at heart, Gutenberg used many different versions

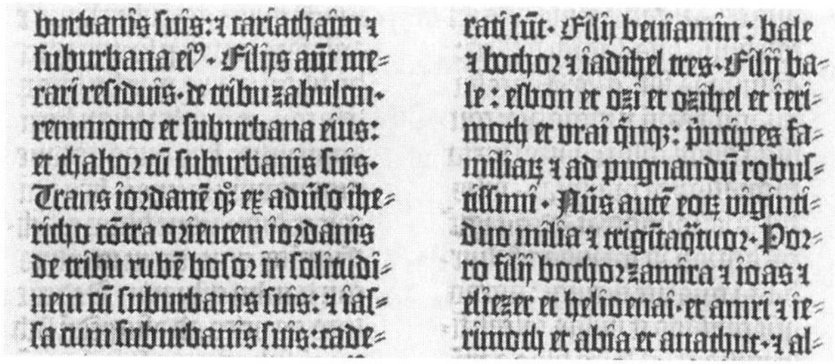

FIGURE 1 Guttenberg Bible with original justification and hyphen use.

of individual letters and was able to subtly stretch and thin letters without making it obvious to the reader. Gutenberg was also fearless in his use of the hyphen; as Keith Houston noted in his book, *Shady Characters,* it was "the most potent weapon at hand in the battle against excessive word spacing" (Houston 130). Whereas scribes before and after Gutenberg would get hung up on rules about hyphen use and where words could be safely broken up (or not), Gutenberg was fiercely adamant that where hyphenation and justification were concerned, there were no rules. Typeset—and the beauty of the page—was king. And Gutenberg would use his arsenal of hyphens to bend the letters and lines to his will.[2]

While hundreds of years later, grammarians such as those writing *The Chicago Manual of Style* would emphasize that hyphenating more than three lines in a row is "undesirable for aesthetic reasons," Gutenberg eschewed those aesthetics, deploying up to eight ladders of consecutive hyphen use.[3] His generous use of the hyphen may have seemed scattershot at first, but Gutenberg revealed his inner perfectionist, adding extra spaces outside the margins of his typeset for double hyphens. It was observed that he set an additional 36,000 characters in order to make room for his beloved hyphen. And while his pursuit of perfection in hyphenation and justification—referred to as H&J's by the book publishing industry today—his perfection has inspired typographers throughout history.

More importantly, Johannes' success had set him free. No longer in the shadow of his father, he had escaped from the ghosts of his family who haunted him. Never again would his father be able to control his destiny. And no longer would Johannes have to resign himself to goldsmithing day in and day out. With the success of his printing press, Johannes turned to writing and printing poetry. Though he is best known for his work on the Bible, for Johannes, the Bible was ultimately a vehicle to achieve his dream of inventing a machine that allowed him to print and memorialize the poems that had been swirling in his mind since he was a young boy.

5 LOST IN MIGRATION

AdeChike felt the weight of his pads and helmet growing heavier on his body. He looked around to see if he could discern if his classmates were as nervous as he was. No luck.

"Ada, Adey, Ada-Chick, Adey—"

"AdeChike, sir," AdeChike said. He fought the urge to look the Coach in the eye and instead kept his gaze lowered. He always dreaded this moment—the first time someone tried to pronounce his name. There were times when AdeChike wanted to swallow the letters, reconfigure them into a more melodious sound.

"Now what the heck kinda name is AdeChike, son?" Coach Samuels said in his southern drawl.

"You can just call me Ade, sir," AdeChike responded, gaze still fixed on the chalk-lined grass in front of him.

"I didn't *ask* what I could call you, *son*," Coach Samuels emphasized the last word causing a shiver to run down AdeChike's spine. "I asked what the heck kinda name that is."

AdeChike swallowed hard. He hated this, but knew it was part of the game.

"It's Yoruba, sir. From Nigeria. My mom is Nigerian," AdeChike responded. He worked hard to make his voice soft, so as to seem less threatening.

"I *know* what Yoruba is, son. You think I was born yesterday?" the coach spat. AdeChike felt his fists clench but tried not to flinch. After all, this man was one of the most powerful men in college football. The coach for the Texas Longhorns, Coach Samuels was AdeChike's ticket out of Lubbock, and his ticket to a better future.

Silence descended on the football field. None of the players moved.

"Well alright then, Yoruba, let's see what you can do, huh?" Samuels said. He picked up his clipboard, straightened his hat and crossed his arms.

AdeChike's high school coach, Coach Carl—a kind man who had been an important father figure for AdeChike throughout his life—nodded at him. AdeChike picked up the football as a few of his fellow players rose from the bench. As soon as they took to the field, AdeChike felt better. Here, he was in his element. Much to his mother's chagrin, the football field was where AdeChike felt most at home. AdeChike played his heart out, elegantly passing the football, launching and catching it at regular intervals. Football was like magic.

The next day AdeChike was home helping his mother in the kitchen when the phone rang. His mother wiped her hands on her apron and picked up the receiver. AdeChike froze as he heard Coach Samuels's booming drawl through the phone.

"Is Adey there?" the coach demanded.

"I don't know anyone by that name," his mother responded, her Nigerian accent still pronounced after all these years of living in Texas. "But if you are looking for my son Ade*Chike*, I can get him for you."

There was a long pause.

"Yes ma'am, that'll be just fine," came the coach's voice.

AdeChike's mother covered the mouthpiece of the receiver and turned to her son with an exasperated expression. "Why you let these people disgrace your beautiful name?"

"Mom!" AdeChike said reaching for the phone. She held it back from him, jaw clenched.

"Your name was chosen by me for who you are. The King of God's strength."

"Mom! Give me the phone, *please*. Now isn't the time," AdeChike begged. His mother handed over the phone with a pronounced eyeroll.

"Hello? This is Ade," he said, avoiding his mother's gaze.

"Well, hello, son. It's Coach Samuels. I'm calling because I have some good news and I want to know when a good time would be to come over to discuss the details." It was more of a proclamation than a question.

AdeChike jumped three feet into the air and pumped his fist.

"Hello? Son? Adey?" came Coach Samuels' voice. AdeChike had almost forgotten about the phone.

"Yes, sir, anytime is fine sir," AdeChike responded.

"Great, I'll be by tomorrow afternoon. See you then."

AdeChike returned the phone to its cradle and turned slowly. He didn't want his mother to ruin the moment for him, but his hopes were dashed quickly.

"I know what you're going to say, Ma," AdeChike started.

"No, not 'Ma,' I am your mother, don't forget that. And you are my son. And I will not have any son of mine going off to play college football. I have let this go on long enough, mostly because I respect and admire Coach Carl, but now, this. I have to put my foot down AdeChike. I must," his mother said. He knew it was bad when her voice dropped several octaves.

"Mom, mother, please, listen to me," AdeChike begged. At six foot two he towered over his mother, but always felt like a little boy in her presence.

"No, AdeChike, *you* listen to *me*," she commanded. AdeChike bit his lip and clenched his fists again as she spoke. "You are my son. And I will *not* have you throwing away your life on that vulgar American sport, you hear me? I will NOT."

"But mom, mother, I *am* American, and I love American football," he protested.

"Shush. You are African. You are not American—you will never be seen as American my child, you hear me? You are a Yoruba man. And you are the living embodiment of your ancestors."

"Mother, please," he begged.

"You think that that disgusting man—that that coach who can't even pronounce your *name*, you think he cares about you? All he wants to do is use you. Use your beautiful body. He doesn't care if you get injured. He doesn't care that you have a perfect brain up in that beautiful head. That you are more than just a fast pair of legs. You are brilliant. But you never let your brilliance shine," his mother continued. He could see tears welling up in her eyes and felt their overwhelming weight throughout his body.

His mother sat at the kitchen table and pulled a cigarette out of her pocket. She lit it and took a long drag. When AdeChike reached for one, she slapped his hand.

"Your brain is more powerful than your body, but don't think I'm going to let you ruin your body," she said. Her voice was lighter this time, so AdeChike ventured a different argument.

"Mother, you know I want to go to college. And you know I want to write—to write poetry. This is my ticket to a really good school. And Austin is supposed to be *the* town for artists and poets. UT is a really good school. And we wouldn't have to pay a single dollar," he said.

His mother shook her head. "You have other options AdeChike. You are a brilliant writer. You'll get into a good school and can focus your time on writing, or maybe even economics? Just no more football, okay?"

"But mom! Who is going to pay for college? Who is going to pay for me to sit around reading books?" AdeChike felt his voice rising and he decided he wouldn't try to control it.

"Watch your tone. And sit back down," his mother commanded. AdeChike's anger continued to build.

"It's not *my* fault we're in this situation. Maybe if you hadn't driven my father away, maybe he would be here and pay for college for me so I wouldn't have to make these choices!" he screamed.

AdeChike's mother took another long drag from her cigarette and exhaled the smoke through her nose. "That was low, AdeChike. Very low. And I know you know that. And don't pretend like you don't love football. You play because you love it, not because you don't have a father to pay for college. I just think it's time you got your priorities straight. A Yoruba man would never dishonor his mother this way—you are losing your way."

AdeChike sensed he wasn't going to get anywhere with his mother. Whenever she clung to their Yoruba traditions, he felt more lost and unsettled.

The next day AdeChike awoke before his mother. He crept downstairs to call first Coach Carl and then Coach Samuels. He had decided the night before that he would meet Coach Samuels at Coach Carl's house instead of running the risk of the Longhorns Coach interfacing with his angry mother. He worried that she would ruin his chances of fulfilling his childhood dream. Both men agreed and AdeChike started up the stairs to find a suitable shirt and tie to wear for the occasion. As he reached the top of the stairs, his mother emerged from her room, her hair tucked into a pink satin nightcap, arms crossed over her beige robe, eyes rimmed red.

"Look Ma, about last night—" AdeChike started.

His mother held up her hand. "I don't want to hear it. Let us never speak of it again. You will not see Coach Samuels and you need to quit the team," she announced.

"WHAT?" AdeChike screamed. "You trying to ruin my life woman?!"

"How *dare* you speak to me that way?" she said, eyes narrowing.

"You know what? You can't control me. I'm eighteen next month," he shot back.

"You will always be my son. Don't be so American. The Yoruba know the bonds of family aren't bound by age" she said. She moved past him to walk down the stairs, clearing her throat to indicate that the conversation was over.

But AdeChike was not ready for the conversation to end. He clenched his fists and walked into his room. He took several deep calming breaths and changed into the only button-down dress shirt he owned—a gift that had appeared some years ago in the mail from a father he hadn't seen since he was three years old.

He walked down the stairs, his braids slicked back, shirt tucked in.

"And where do you think you're going?" his mother barked.

"I'm leaving Mother. I'm taking the car and going to Coach Carl's house, so you can walk to work today," he announced. Before she had a chance to respond, AdeChike walked out, slamming the front door as he left.

When he returned home later that day his mother was nowhere to be found. As the day gave way to night, AdeChike wondered where she was and decided to drive to the Wal-Mart where she worked. When he walked in, the manager rushed up to him and asked if he knew where his mother was.

He didn't. It was raining and he wondered if she had decided not to walk to work in the rain. But then, where was she?

When he returned home, she still had not appeared. Around 10 p.m. the kitchen phone rang again. Startled, AdeChike ran to pick it up.

The voice on the other end of the phone was deep and oddly familiar.

"Is this AdeChike?" a gruff male voice asked.

"Who wants to know?" AdeChike returned.

"It's me, champ. It's your father."

Silence.

"Look, I'm calling because . . . well, I'm calling . . . " His father was stumbling.

AdeChike's stomach sank. Something was wrong. Why else was his erstwhile absent father calling him?

"There isn't any easy way to say this Ade," he continued.

"It's AdeChike, you know that," AdeChike corrected him sharply.

"Right, AdeChike. Look, I'm calling because, because, well, look. It's your mother. She was hit by a car earlier today and . . . and . . . I'm afraid she didn't make it," the voice said. His father was stoic.

AdeChike sank to the floor clutching the phone. Tears sprang to his eyes and he dug his fingernails into his skin. He tried to respond, but couldn't.

"Look, it's a lot, I know. I'll drive out to Texas in the morning. Just sit tight, I'll be there soon," his father said.

AdeChike hung up the phone and ran to the sink to vomit.

6 LIKE WATER FOR CHOCOLATE

The rich aroma of chocolate and spices filled the kitchen as Ania stirred the molé, careful not to let the edges burn in her mother's cast-iron pot. She cleaned the chicken breasts and turned to chopping the onions, letting the tears flow from her eyes with every cut. Each time she chopped onions she felt like Tita, the main character in her favorite book *Like Water for Chocolate*, or, as she insisted on referring to it, *Como Agua Para Chocolate*. She had watched the cooking scenes from the movie over and over, practicing how Esquivel's characters rolled letters off their tongues.

"And what exactly are you doing?" came her mother's voice, snapping Ania out of her reverie.

Ania wiped the tears from her eyes, careful to use her wrist so as not to get any traces of onion on her face. She sniffled.

"Are you crying?" her mother demanded.

"Mami, as Tita says, 'the problem with crying while chopping the onions isn't the crying, it's that sometimes one starts crying and can't stop.'"

"Don't call me *Mami*. Mom or mother, you know that. And there you go, quoting that stupid movie again," her mother said.

"Book, mom," Ania interjected.

"Whatever. And are you making chicken with that chocolate sauce again?" her mom asked.

"It's Mami, you know what it is and how to say it, it's *mole*," Ania corrected her mother. Her mother rolled her eyes.

"I wish you would snap out of it Ania," her mother said.

"Snap out of what? My culture? Who I am? A proud *Mexicana?*" Ania shot back.

"You're American now, don't forget that."

"I'd rather forget," Ania snapped back. "Plus, it's technically your fault, all of this."

Ania could tell her mother wasn't sure exactly what her daughter was accusing her of.

When Ania was only three years old, her mother had fled violence in their hometown of Oaxaca de Juarez, the capital of the state of Oaxaca, and crossed the border into southern Arizona. Along with her two older brothers, Ania had grown up in a small town near the border.

When Ania was young, her mother worked as a cleaning lady, and would bring her daughter along with her to clean many of the houses at which she worked. While her mom vacuumed or did laundry, Ania would sneak into the rooms of the owners' young children to read their books. For a time, she had been enamored with the *Junie B Jones* series, following the young protagonist on misadventures and living vicariously through Junie's confidence in challenging the adults in her life. Then Ania started following *Ramona Quimby* and later the *Harry Potter* series. But something always felt missing in all of these books: none of them featured heroes or heroines who looked or sounded like her.

Sure, she could relate to Hermione Granger's smarts, Ramona Quimby's practicality, and Junie B Jones' sense of adventure, but why wasn't she, Ania, reflected in any of these pages? Where were the Mexican queens, the Venezuelan princesses, the Columbian heroes?

When she was ten years old, Ania accompanied her mother to the home of a new employer. She was disappointed to find that the house hosted no children, searching various rooms for any sign of children's books and finding nothing. An hour into her search she stumbled into a home office; there she found several bookcases filled with colorful and interesting-sounding books. But one stood out—a bright blue cover with an Oaxacan painting on the front. She pulled at the spine and the book tumbled into her hands. *Like Water for Chocolate* by Laura Esquivel. Ania could barely contain her excitement as she turned the pages of this sumptuous book. Here was something she could sink her teeth into, here was a book that tickled all of her senses and made her feel alive!

When her mother had finished cleaning the house, she called to Ania from the front door and announced it was time to go home. Only half-way through the book, Ania could not bear to part with her newfound treasure. She bit her lip as she stuffed the book up her shirt and pulled her sweater closed shut. She hesitated for a moment before heading to the door. If her mother found out that she had stolen something from a client she would be furious. But, on the other hand, how could Ania *not* take this book home? After all, this book was practically speaking directly to her—calling her. She crossed her arms over her chest, clutching the book closer to her body as she slunk out of the house and climbed into her mother's car. She didn't speak to her mother the whole way home out of fear that she would be caught.

Her mother had taken her silence as a symbol of her daughter's enduring anger. Earlier that year Ania's mother had come home one evening with a tall stranger. This man, named Robert, was introduced as their father-to-be. While her brothers had stormed out of the house, Ania had just stood there, studying the man—his straight blonde hair and crystal blue eyes a sharp contrast to everything she loved about her mother, from her thick curling black hair to her warm brown eyes. Even worse, Robert did not speak any Spanish, and from that day on, her mother had banned anyone in the family from speaking their native tongue. The ultimate insult, in Ania's eyes, was that Robert robbed them of their culture.

Ania's mother stopped cooking Oaxacan food, instead favoring dishes she knew Robert preferred like meatloaf or pasta primavera. At night, Ania could hear her mother working to rid herself of her Spanish accent. Over the years, Ania's mother would struggle with this task, but, in an ironic twist of fate, Ania was the first to lose her native tongue, being the youngest member of the family. By the time she was thirteen she would remember only the few words of Spanish she pried out of her favorite book, *Como Agua Para Chocolate.*

It wasn't until some years after Ania's transgression that her mother discovered what her daughter had done. She was cleaning Ania's room and found the book under her daughter's bed, pages folded and bent, and the front tattered. By that point, their relationship had become so painfully strained that her mother's anger had little bearing on Ania.

Ania's mother had married Robert before Ania's eleventh birthday, and, by then, had changed almost everything about herself, becoming almost unrecognizable to her children. She had changed the pronunciation of her first name from Claudia pronounced as *Cl-OW-dia* (the Spanish pronunciation) to the Anglicized *Claadia,* with the middle syllable seemingly swallowed. When her mother announced that she was changing her last name to Smith to match her husband's, Ania had refused to change hers, clinging onto Lopez fiercely. And while her mother insisted on introducing her daughter with an Anglicized version of her last name, Ania would often correct her mother and others with the Spanish pronunciation. Much to her mother's chagrin, she continued to seek out books written by Mexican or Mexican-American authors, plunging into an imagined adolescence that Ania felt had been taken from her by her mother's choices not only to leave Mexico, but to erase their culture by marrying Robert.

Over the course of Ania's teenage years, she and her mother grew further and further apart. When Ania enrolled herself in Spanish classes in high school, her mother pulled her out and insisted her daughter enroll in French instead. Whenever Ania had the chance to do research about her family and culture for a school project, she and her mother would fight.

"Why can't you just let it go Ania?" her mother would say in exasperation.

"Let my culture go? What are you asking me Mami? To get whitewashed like you?" Ania would shoot back.

Back and forth the two would argue. Ania's mother insisting that her daughter was American, Ania insisting she was Oaxacan. Ania criticized her mother when she became the CEO of a cleaning business for becoming too capitalistic and corporate. Ania's mother criticized her daughter for her choice in food, clothing, and her insistence on decorating her room like it was always *el Dia de los Muertos*.

By the time she was eighteen, Ania couldn't wait to move to Phoenix to attend Arizona State University. Her mother had been reluctant to support her daughter's decision to go to college, mostly because she found out through reading her application that her daughter planned to double-major in Transborder Studies and Chicana History. That summer was the last time Ania and her mother would live under the same roof, and rather than be a time to enjoy one another, the two had been bickering almost non-stop.

While they fought, the *molé* sauce simmered, and was now threatening to boil over. Ania quickly turned off the stove and then spun around to face her mother.

Ania stood there in the kitchen, her favorite room in their house, and held her mother's gaze defiantly. Her mother walked over to the stove and spooned some of Ania's *mole* into her mouth gingerly.

"Hm," she said, her black eyebrows knitting together. Though her mother had been dying her hair lighter and lighter each year, she usually forgot her eyebrows, something for which Ania was grateful. Her brows and the rich chocolate brown of her mother's eyes were among the most visceral reminders of their culture.

"This sauce," she said, avoiding the word *molé* deliberately. "It doesn't even taste good. You see, Ania, you're not even a good Oaxacan cook. Maybe stick to cupcakes, okay?" Her mother turned on her heel and walked out the door. Ania returned to her onions, allowing the flood of tears to take her over.

PART 2

HYPHEN AS DIVIDER

7 SCOLDING PRIVATE HYPHEN

The hyphenated American is ridiculous. But that's what we have to put up with. I think that any person that's in the United States is better off here than they would be where they came from.

—JOHN WAYNE

In the summer of 1915, former President Teddy Roosevelt was struggling. He had just returned from a two-year expedition to the Amazon in South America where he nearly died collecting specimens to bring back for the American Museum of Natural History. He had decided to take his father's advice to go to the Amazon following his defeat in the presidential race of 1912, when he was beat out by Woodrow Wilson. Roosevelt had been certain that by entering the race against the incumbent William Taft that he had a strong shot at winning back the presidency. Initially a mentor of Taft's, he had grown gradually disenchanted with what he viewed as Taft's conservatism.

In the months leading up to the election of 1912, Roosevelt had convinced himself that he was the savior not only of the Republican party, but of America and Americanism in general. He believed that he knew the true potential of American progressivism, and that Taft was wasting the presidency. Thus, he decided to run against his former mentee, but the two men ended up splitting the Republican vote causing Woodrow Wilson to win the presidency. Angry at this turn of events, Roosevelt decided to walk out on the Republicans and found what would come to be known as the "Bull Moose Party" in late 1912. But Roosevelt still felt restless.

It was this restlessness which inspired him to accept an invitation to the South American Amazon where he would lead an expedition to explore, interestingly, the trail of the River of Doubt in the Amazon Basin, which was renamed after the former President as Rio Roosevelt following the expedition. But the trip was challenging from the start. Many members of Roosevelt's crew suffered from malaria and other insect-borne diseases. In addition to a gash on his leg that nearly killed him, and several other unidentifiable diseases, it is said that Roosevelt also experienced feelings of alienation as an outsider in the Amazon. He had hoped to be traveling to Brazil and Argentina on a victory tour after winning the presidency, but this decidedly less-glamorous visit, along with Roosevelt's lack of Portuguese language, weighed heavily on him, making the trip all the more unbearable.

By the time he returned to the United States in 1914, angry and determined, the First World War was in full force, and Roosevelt found himself launching a campaign of critique against Wilson's hesitancy to enter the war. Roosevelt was vocal in his support of the Allies and demanded harsh policies against Germany and German war tactics. He grew increasingly infuriated with Wilson's foreign policies, referring to the president as a failure. He was emphatic that Americans needed to express their loyalties, and joined the wave of anti-hyphenism that was sweeping the nation.

Between 1890 and 1920, the epithet "hyphenated American" came into use to bolster the xenophobia that accompanied the second wave of immigration to the United States. Referring to the hyphen between the name of an ethnicity and the word "American," hyphenism and hyphenated Americanism was seen as a potentially fracturing and divisive force in an America on the brink of war. Irish-Americans, German-Americans and Jewish-Americans were among the first to be pinpointed by this xenophobia, though the discrimination extended to Chinese-Americans and others as well. The term "hyphenated American" condemned those who identified as anything other than American who would raise concerns about American allegiance, especially against the Germans in the First World War. As leaders like Roosevelt pushed the United States to join the Allies in the First World War, the loyalty of German-Americans (as well as other recent immigrants such as Italian-Americans) was called into question.

It was within this context, and on the heels of his fury about losing the election, anxieties about losing his country, and after returning from an essentially failed expedition, that Roosevelt penned a speech to be delivered on October 12th—in honor of Columbus Day—of 1915 to the Catholic Fraternal Organization, the Knights of Columbus.[1] This group was known for advocating the cause of equity and justice, and Roosevelt decided to use the occasion of this speech to make his bold proclamation about hyphenated Americans that would go down in history, and mark a turning point in how the hyphen became demonized both orthographically and politically. The following passages from his speech are noteworthy in that these words echoed throughout history, emboldening xenophobia against hyphenated individuals for decades to come.

There is no room in this country for hyphenated Americanism. When I refer to hyphenated Americans, I do not refer to naturalized Americans. Some of the very best Americans I have ever known were naturalized Americans, Americans born abroad. But a hyphenated American is not an American at all. This is just as true of the man who puts "native" before the hyphen as of the man who puts German or Irish or English or French before the hyphen. Americanism is a matter of the spirit and of the soul. Our allegiance must be purely to the United States. We must unsparingly condemn any man who holds any other allegiance. But if he is heartily and singly loyal to this Republic, then no matter where he was born, he is just as good an American as any one else.

The one absolutely certain way of bringing this nation to ruin, of preventing all possibility of its continuing to be a nation at all, would be to permit it to become a tangle of squabbling nationalities, an intricate knot of German-Americans, Irish-Americans, English-Americans, French-Americans, Scandinavian-Americans or Italian-Americans, each preserving its separate nationality, each at heart feeling more sympathy with Europeans of that nationality, than with the other citizens of the American Republic. The men who do not become Americans and nothing else are hyphenated Americans; and there ought to be no room for them in this country. The man who calls himself an American citizen and who yet shows by his actions that he is primarily the citizen of a foreign land, plays a thoroughly mischievous part in the life of our body politic. He has no place here; and the sooner he returns to the land to which he feels his real heart-allegiance, the better it will be for every good American. There is no such thing as a hyphenated American who is a good American. The only man who is a good American is the man who is an American and nothing else . . .

For an American citizen to vote as a German-American, an Irish-American, or an English-American, is to be a traitor to American institutions; and those hyphenated Americans who terrorize American politicians by threats of the foreign vote are engaged in treason to the American Republic . . .[2]

The speech was as much a political proclamation as it was an orthographic command. The hyphen had to be removed as it had been sutured to the idea of "un-Americanism." And while it was borne of a moment of frustration in an attempt to take a jab at his opponent, Woodrow Wilson, it reverberated throughout history, and Roosevelt's words continued to appear as refrains.

Interestingly, Wilson, the object of Roosevelt's intense critique, also became an anti-hyphenate himself. In his "Final Address in Support of the League of Nations," Wilson famously said "Any man who carries a hyphen about with him carries a dagger that he is ready to plunge into the vitals of this Republic whenever he gets ready."[3]

In the lead up to the Second World War, The Japanese American Citizens League debated over the usage of the hyphen, concerned that the use of "Japanese" acted as a noun in the hyphenated "Japanese-American," which might perpetuate the notion of divided Japanese American (note no hyphen) loyalty during the Second World War.

Because of this overwhelmingly negative characterization and because of the weight of the associations with hyphenated Americanism, grammar sources such as the *Chicago Manual of Style* encouraged writers to drop the hyphen when referring to any immigrants.[4] In one edition of the *Oxford English Dictionary* the second entry of "hyphenated" reads: "Applied to persons (or, by extension, their activities) born in one country but naturalized citizens of another, their nationality being designated by a hyphenated form, e.g. Anglo-American,

Irish-American; hence, to a person whose *patriotic allegiance is assumed to be divided*" (emphasis mine).[5]

The nail on the coffin came when John Wayne crooned his popular lyric "The Hyphen" following the Second World War. John Wayne's song was a sign of the anti-hyphenating times that he was living in. He was one of many anti-immigrant/anti-hyphenated American public figures whose destructive utterings led to negative feelings nationwide about the hyphen and hyphenated Americans. Here was the ultimate symbol of American masculinity boldly proclaiming Roosevelt's words in song: A hyphenated American could not be an American after all.

> The hyphen, Webster's Dictionary defines,
> Is a symbol used to divide a
> compound word or a single word.
> So it seems to me that when a man calls himself
> An "Afro-American," a "Mexican-American," "Italian-American,"
> An "Irish-American," "Jewish-American,"
> What he's sayin' is, "I'm a divided American."
> Well, we all came from other places,
> Different creeds and different races,
> To form a nation . . . to become as one.
> Yet look at the harm a line has done—
> A simple little line, and yet
> As divisive as a line can get.[6]

8 PARDIS 9/11

Someone had left the small 1980s style television on in the corner of our make-shift newsroom. Only two of us were in the office on that eerily quiet New York City morning in September of 2001.

Kareem and I were co-editors of *Slant Magazine,* a recently popularized New York publication that we produced from our perch as graduate students at Columbia University. Aspiring journalists and expert journalism professors from Columbia journalism school, as well as a range of other schools at the institution regularly contributed essays, and Kareem and I had the difficult task of choosing and rejecting. That the magazine was run by me, an Iranian-American woman, and Kareem, an Arab-American man, had not, up until that point, been of problematic significance, but a lot of things were about to change that day.

I was struggling with a piece on identity politics in Brazil when I looked up at the television screen. While others looked out the window to clear their brains, I preferred the TV, because it allowed me to finally turn my constantly chattering brain off. As my eyes floated up to the screen in the corner, I squinted to make sense of what I was seeing. A grey airplane crashing into one of the twin towers of the World Trade Center.

"Hey Kareem, did someone change the channel from the news? Like, is this a blockbuster movie I must have missed?" I asked, confused.

Kareem spun his chair around to face the TV. I watched his eyes widen.

"What the fu— turn the volume up," he said.

"What movie is this?" I asked, still unable to process what I was seeing.

"This isn't a movie, P, this is CNN," Kareem said as he stood and floated over to the screen. I was standing from my desk now to get a better look at the visuals. We both stood staring in disbelief. Could this be happening?

Kareem crossed his arms behind his head. "Is this really happening?" he asked rhetorically.

A few minutes passed. And then, unbelievably, we watched the screen as another plane hit the second tower. I heard myself screaming before I realized the sound was coming from my mouth.

"Holy shit, holy shit!" Kareem said, his fingers by now digging into his scalp as he paced the room. We both opened our cell phones at the same exact time—I was dialing my parents in California, he his mother in Cairo.

I had forgotten about the time difference and only realized it when I heard my mother's sleepy voice on the other end of the phone.

"Mommy?" I said softly. She groaned an almost inaudible response.

"Mommy, I'm sorry to have woken you," I said, switching to Persian. I didn't know then that I had limited time on the phone, but something told me to switch to her native tongue so her sleepy brain could really comprehend what I was about to say next.

"Mommy, I'm okay all right? I'm okay," I said.

"What are you talking about? Why wouldn't you be okay?" she said.

"Something bad has happened in New York. Turn on the news. But remember, I'm—" and then the phone was cut off.

Kareem hadn't been able to reach his mother, as his cell phone had stopped working minutes before mine. He reached for the landline, nearly tripping over the tangled mess of cords in our editing room. He held the receiver to his ear with his chin. His right hand clicked the phone buttons to get a dial tone, while his left hand steered his mouse to see if the internet was still working.

"No dial tone?" I asked, hoping what I was saying wasn't true. Kareem shook his head and my stomach sank.

"This is going to be really bad, Pardis, you understand? This is going to be really bad for a lot of people like you and me. Get it?" he said. I shook my head. I didn't get it. I wouldn't get it for several more hours, but Kareem knew then that regardless of who was behind this act of terror, that we—Muslims—would be blamed. We were, after all, living in George W. Bush's America, just months before he would deliver his "Axis of Evil" speech.

That day changed the lives of so many people around the world. In New York City alone, people would grieve for months if not years over the pain they experienced. For me, the grief and fear took a different shape. Rather than share the anxieties of my roommates or friends who feared another attack, I was most afraid when I left the house to go to the grocery store, or when I rode the metro. I was scared not of another attack, but frightened that people would look at me, figure out I was Muslim and Middle Eastern, and react badly. These fears did come to fruition on several occasions in Manhattan, when people would deliberately bump into me or give me dirty looks. I made certain that I never spoke in Persian on the phone or with my Iranian friends in New York. And when my father arrived three weeks later to celebrate my birthday with me, I insisted we stay home for a quiet dinner rather than run the risk of being seen eating out, worried people would overhear my father's accent.

Perhaps the worst incident that exacerbated my fears was when I finally gathered the courage to travel. It was Thanksgiving, a few months after 9/11, and my parents had insisted my brother Paymohn and I come home for the holiday. But we were nervous about flying. I instructed my brother to wear a baseball cap with a local team name on it and purchased for myself a Polo shirt with the American flag emblazoned across the chest.

"We're Americans!" I wanted to scream at the TSA agent who put us in a separate line and strip searched us. "We love baseball and American pie!" I wanted to announce to everyone waiting at the gate for our flight. I wanted to tell everyone that we had no divided loyalties—that we were also grieving the tragedy of 9/11, that we knew who the bad guys were and that we didn't identify with them.

As we boarded the plane, my brother kept his face down, hands in his pockets. He hunched over, curling into himself as though he wanted to disappear. For my part, I had somehow come up with a southern accent, as if to prove my American-ness. I adopted a drawl to emphasize how good an American I was. And I had been using "Patty" as my Starbucks name since that fateful morning in September. Little did I know that these were habits I would take with me for decades.

Once the plane took off, my brother removed his baseball cap and slipped it into his backpack. At a certain point he wanted to get up to use the bathroom. As he had the window seat and I the middle, I stood to allow him to pass. I turned to face my fellow passengers on the plane, and watched their eyes lock on my brother, a six-foot-tall, dark skinned Iranian man with a five o'clock shadow. I saw their faces go white. When he walked calmly toward the back of the plane and everyone realized he was just using the bathroom, I watched dozens of people visibly exhale. This was going to be our life from now on. Kareem was right.

I spent the next five years in Manhattan finishing up my PhD in Anthropology at Columbia. At that time, I learned to, in the words of Margaret Mead, "make the strange familiar, and the familiar strange." Yet at the same time, I was also actively working to erase my Iranian-ness in ways that made those around me feel more comfortable; but those ways also made me hate myself.

After two years of suffocating my Iranian side, I swung in the opposite direction: I became more involved with the Muslim Students Association and began spending time with former Black Panthers. We organized anti-war protests and sit-ins, and I began writing about identity politics in the era of the "Axis of Evil."[1]

I'll never forget the White, male professor who publicly humiliated me in class after I had turned in an essay on the unbearable weight of Islam post-9/11, in which I used the work of Malcom X and Frantz Fannon to explain what Iranian and Arab-Americans were experiencing in post-9/11 New York.

"You think you have anything in common with the Black power movement?" he asked. "I mean are you really comparing yourself to what Black people experienced? I mean Arabs aren't really people of color you know. And Iranians, aren't you the original Aryans?" I left class and burst into tears in the bathroom.

Later, a Moroccan-American classmate named Mouna whom I had met briefly but never spoken with came to find me.

"You know what is hard?" she said to me, handing me a lit cigarette and leaning out the bathroom window to watch the traffic on Amsterdam and 118th street grind to a halt. I joined her at the window, squeezing my torso through and tilting my chin up, partly to encourage her to continue and partly to avoid blowing smoke in her face.

"It's like this," Mouna continued. "We aren't considered *real* women of color unless we are. In some settings we are seen as not 'of color' enough—like what happened to you in class today. And I get it, our struggles are nowhere near what Black women or other marginalized folks experience. But it is still the case that when people see us, they feel fear or anxiety. Especially after *it* happened," she said. "So, we are read as people of color when they want to fear us, but then excluded from the movements of solidarity, and not 'counted' as people of color in a lot of settings where it does matter."

I would come back to that conversation many years later when interviewing for a position as a Dean. A search consultant would ask me to justify why I stated that I was a woman of color. I would rehearse the same words that Mouna said that day, nuanced over decades of thought, but always in my arsenal of weapons to deploy in code switching. Having the language to explain the oppression I carried would help me bridge to other hyphenated and non-hyphenated individuals alike.

9 ADE

"So, tell me young man," the reporter began condescendingly. "How long exactly have you been a Black running back?"

AdeChike was confused. He lifted his hands and looked at the dark skin stretching over his cracked knuckles. Was this a trick question?

"Mr. Thompson, my son is not a *Black* running back" AdeChike's father interjected. Lately, his father had taken to accompanying him on all his interviews with the press. Ade wondered if his father was trying to censor him or attempting to live vicariously through him. "He is an All-Star, All-American Athlete."

Ade sat up straighter and wiped the sweat from his brow. Growing up in Texas he could not fathom a place hotter than Lubbock, but sure enough, Phoenix was hotter. Little did he know that when his father had arrived in Lubbock for his mother's funeral, his life would continue to spin out of his hands. Temperature would be the least of his worries.

"Sorry Mr. Ellis," the reporter responded. He put his pen down, turned off the voice recorder, and shifted somewhat anxiously in his seat. It seemed to AdeChike that Mr. Thompson was suddenly uncomfortable in the presence of two tall Black men, because he sat up straighter and deepened his voice. "It's just that we don't see that many Black first-year kids starting in college ball you know?"

"Kellen Mond, Jamie Newman, Jalen Hurts, Tyler Huntley, Justin Fields," AdeChike said, avoiding the reporter's eyes. He found that if he didn't look white men in the eyes, they would feel more comfortable around him. And while he hated doing this, he felt it important that the reporter hear what he was saying.

"Excuse me?" Mr. Thompson said.

"Black quarterbacks starting in college ball," AdeChike said, now looking directly into the reporter's eyes.

"Right," the reporter said. Now he looked down to avoid eye contact with the father-son duo who sat across from him in the empty box of Sun Devil Stadium. Mr. Thompson picked up his pad and paper and began scribbling.

"Uh, and 19 years," AdeChike added. He felt emboldened suddenly by the reporter's shifting body language. It signaled an opening. But, from the corner of his right eye he could see his father's jaw clench.

The reporter stopped writing and looked up in confusion. "Sorry, come again son?"

"19 years," AdeChike responded, now feeling his jaws clench. "You asked how long I've been a *Black* running back. I'm 19 years old, and as far as I know, I came out of my mother's womb Black. And I actually consider myself

African-American. You know, to honor my roots. Oh, and I'm not your son."

"Ah, right," Mr. Thompson responded. He picked up his pen to write, then put it down. There was an uncomfortable silence in the room.

"I'm sorry about my son, Mr. Thompson," AdeChike's father jumped back in. "He's just stressed. Nervous about the big game with USC coming up. That's all, he didn't mean anything by it." AdeChike could sense that he was going to get an earful from his father as soon as Mr. Thompson disappeared, but he didn't care.

"Right, right. Of course, of course, I understand," Mr. Thompson said. He shifted again and began packing up his belongings. "Well, Go Devils and all that. Good luck at the big game, Ade."

"It's Ade*Chike*," AdeChike emphasized looking straight at the reporter. He watched the man finish packing his bags and hurry out to the stands.

When the reporter was out of eyesight, AdeChike's father turned to his son angrily.

"What is your problem, Ade? That was a really messed up thing you did," he said. His tone was icy. AdeChike got up and stretched his legs. He loosened his tie and began taking off the button-down white shirt his father insisted he wear for all his interviews. He hated the suffocating shirt almost as much as he hated his suffocating father.

As if losing his mother wasn't bad enough, his father had shown up and announced that AdeChike would be coming to live with him in Phoenix. For the first few weeks after his mother's death, AdeChike had been numb. He recalled telling Coach Carl that he would never play football again at his mother's funeral. AdeChike was convinced that her death was a result of his love for the game. Coach Carl said he understood and transmitted the message back to the coaches of the Longhorns as well as several other Texas college football coaches who had expressed interest in AdeChike joining their team.

At first, AdeChike had been so distraught that he hadn't noticed the absence of football, the community of players who had become like his family, the structure of his daily life, and the gentle guidance provided by Coach Carl. He reluctantly agreed to move to Arizona with his father, learning about the man who felt like a complete stranger as they made the drive.

He learned that his father was a war veteran. He had been deployed to Iraq during Operation Desert Storm, and he considered this his highest achievement.

"Defending America and her great values is the greatest achievement," his father would say to him repeatedly. When AdeChike would push back on his father, insisting that America had a sordid history when it came to Africa, echoing his mother's words, his father quickly became angry.

"I don't want to hear anything like that from any son of mine, you hear?" he would say. "We are Americans. That's it. Not 'African-Americans,' not Black. We are Americans. And we are as American as anyone else in this country."

Worse still, his father had insisted on shortening his name to Ade. He would insist on his son introducing himself as Ade Ellis, as he felt this would help him fit in in Arizona.

"I never had trouble fitting in in Texas, so why would Arizona be any different?" AdeChike asked his father as they crossed the state line into Arizona on their long drive to his father's house. "Plus, I'm not *just* American—I'm as much African as American. My name is my heritage. I carry the Yoruba spirits of my ancestors, like mother always said."

"I don't want to hear any more talk of that. You know what the great General Schwarzkopf said? He said 'A hyphenated American is not an American at all,'" AdeChike's father shot back.

"I'm pretty sure it was Roosevelt who said that. And not during Desert Storm either," AdeChike muttered. AdeChike recalled that as the first time his father raised his hand on him—but it wouldn't be the last. This clarified for AdeChike that he and his father were and would remain from different worlds.

AdeChike grabbed his gym bag and headed downstairs into the locker room. It was moments like these that made him glad that he hadn't given up on football in the end. When he had first moved to Phoenix with his father, he decided to forego college and football altogether. He got a job at one of Phoenix's many golf courses, caddying for wealthy men who fueled AdeChike's anger toward Phoenix, toward Arizona, toward the world in general. But after a year of caddying, coming home to a father who seldom acknowledged his presence, AdeChike yearned for the life he felt had been cut short.

One afternoon while caddying at the golf course, one of his regular clients asked him if he wanted to attend the ASU homecoming football game. They would be playing their long-time rivals, the University of Arizona Wildcats. AdeChike was unsure at first, but when he was handed two free tickets, he accepted, called the one friend he had made working at the golf course, and headed to Sun Devil Stadium on a warm November afternoon.

That day changed everything. Just walking into the stadium ignited something inside him that he thought had died along with his mother. He felt a lightness, a sense of intoxication, of pure joy. He was enthralled in every second of the game. The next day he called Coach Carl to ask for his advice. Before he knew it, his former coach had set up an interview for AdeChike with ASU's head football coach, Herm Edwards. Three months later he was not only accepted to ASU with a full scholarship, but a starting player on the offensive team. For the first time in months, his father took interest in him, and began attending all of AdeChike's practices and games, insisting that everyone call his son Ade.

As AdeChike made his way to the locker room, his phone buzzed in his pocket. He fished it out to see that his roommate, Zach, had texted him three or four times. Zach was often trying to get AdeChike to go to a protest or student activist forums. He always told Zach he didn't have time; although some part of him usually wanted to go, he was afraid of losing the balance of his current life, and the life he was working to achieve. His father had managed to convince him that he couldn't play college ball—the one thing that made him happy—if he got involved in politics. But increasingly it felt to AdeChike like he was splitting his passions—his soul—into two.

When AdeChike walked into the locker room, a group of the guys were huddled in a circle on the floor. At first, he thought they were stretching, but as he drew closer, he realized they were sitting very still, deeply enmeshed in conversation.

"Ade, you're here now. Good. Right on time," Darius said looking up. Darius was one of the fastest tight ends in college football, a junior at ASU. He was the one who had convinced Ade to take classes in African and African-American Studies in the School of Social Transformation at ASU.

"What's up, team?" Ade asked. He threw his gym bag to the floor with a thud and started fiddling with the diamond studs in his ears. His mother had given him the earrings as an early graduation present just weeks before the accident.

"We'll be taking a knee at the big game this weekend right man?" Darius said. The other guys looked at Ade to discern a response. He was the newest member of the starting team, but knew that the others often looked to him for cues. Ade wasn't sure what to do. He silently looked from Darius to his teammates.

"Right, Ade?" said Jefferson, another teammate. "Or is that giant pic of Kap in your room just for show?"

AdeChike had idolized Colin Kaepernick since his childhood. It was one of the few things on which he and his mother agreed. In the rare moments when she supported him playing football, she would tell him that she hoped her son would turn out half as good as "that Colin boy." Kaepernick, or Kap as they all called him, had become increasingly political and politicized in the movement for Black Lives. As a result, Ade's father had torn down the poster that Ade initially put up in his room, but his roommate Zach had bought him a new one for his birthday knowing how much that would mean to him.

AdeChike wanted more than anything to take a knee at the game. But he knew it was risky. Being overtly political might jeopardize his standing as a player, and, worse, would incur the wrath of his father. Ade needed to talk to Zach; he needed his roommates even perspective.

As it happened, when Zach answered Ade's call, he was on his way to an event at the School of Social Transformation (SST). Zach told his roommate to join him at the event which was an examination of intersectional identity politics.

"I need to talk to you about taking a knee," Ade begged.

"Finally, my friend. Finally," Zach responded. He had become actively involved in several student movements as part of the Rainbow Coalition. And Zach was always trying to release his roommates' inner activist.

"Can't you just meet me at our spot?" Ade asked.

"You need to get your ass over here to SST, you're gonna wanna hear what this new Director is saying," Zach said. He hung up and Ade joined him a few moments later.

I saw Ade walk into the room from my vantage point at the microphone. I recognized him from the football games I had attended, and I had seen him occasionally walking the halls on his way to one of the professors offices in the African and African-American Studies wing. He caught my eye and I nodded at an open seat in the front. I could tell he was scanning the room for familiar faces and wasn't sure if he had found any.

"Every American is a hyphenated American," I said, continuing my speech. "We need to embrace the power within the hyphen itself."

I watched Ade flinch. He looked at me like something had landed on him.

After the talk ended, I watched Ade join one of my research assistants, Zach. Zach was one of our best students in the LGBT certificate program, and he had been the one to introduce me to the main student activist forum, the Council of Coalitions. He was also involved with a new student group called "Devils in the Bedroom."

"You made it," I overheard Zach say to Ade. Ade bumped fists with Zach and a few other students who were gathered in the corner enjoying refreshments.

Ade walked up to me and introduced himself. "Could I come see you some time, Prof?" he asked me shyly. I told him I looked forward to it.

"I'm dragging him to the Coalitions meeting tonight," Zach told me. I nodded in approval. "He's been resisting it, because he knows he'll fall in love with the Black African Coalition," Zach continued.

"They do have a good name," Ade said. He paused and then looked at me, "if only there were a hyphen in it?"

10 A HYPHEN SET IN STONE

In the midst of an unusually hot New York City Spring in 1945, Chief Magistrate Henry H. Curran was riding the metro downtown to a meeting at City Hall. Curran, the former Commissioner of Immigration at the Port of New York, and former President of the Association Against the Prohibition Amendment, had forgotten to bring his copy of the paper that morning. As a result, he found himself reading the various ads surrounding him on the colorful New York City subway.

Curran tried to focus on different advertisements to distract himself from the heat, and from his growing restlessness. Until, that is, one particular ad seized his attention. It was an ad for the "New-York Historical Society." Innocuous enough at first, it was the tiny piece of orthography that caught Curran's eye and sent a wave of heat through his body. Was that—could that be a hyphen? Sitting unabashedly between the words "New" and "York?" The anti-hyphenate politician was furious.[1]

Curran swiftly exited the subway, marched into City Hall and got his friend, President of the New York City Council, Newbold Morris, on the phone. Later that week, The *New York World-Telegram*—oh, the irony of the hyphen placement in the publication that reported the incident—documented the conversation between Morris and Curran.

"This thing—this hyphen—is like a gremlin which sneaks around in the dark . . . you should call a special meeting of City Council immediately and have a surgical operation on it! We won't be hyphenated by anyone!" Curran reportedly said to Morris.

What Curran either didn't know, or wanted to erase, was the fact that up until the late 1890s, cities like "New-York" and "New-Jersey" were usually hyphenated to be consistent with other phrases that had both a noun and an adjective. In 1804, when the "New-York Historical Society" was founded, therefore, hyphenation was *de rigueur*. The practice of hyphenating New York was adhered to in books and newspapers, and adopted by other states. Even the *New York Times* featured a masthead written as *The New-York Times* until the late 1890s.

It was only when the pejorative phrasing of "hyphenated Americans" came into vogue in the 1890s, emboldened by Roosevelt's anti-hyphen speech, that the pressure for the hyphen's erasure came to pass.

Curran was no exception to the wave of anti-immigrant xenophobia sweeping the nation at the time of Roosevelt's speech and in the lead up to the First and Second World Wars.

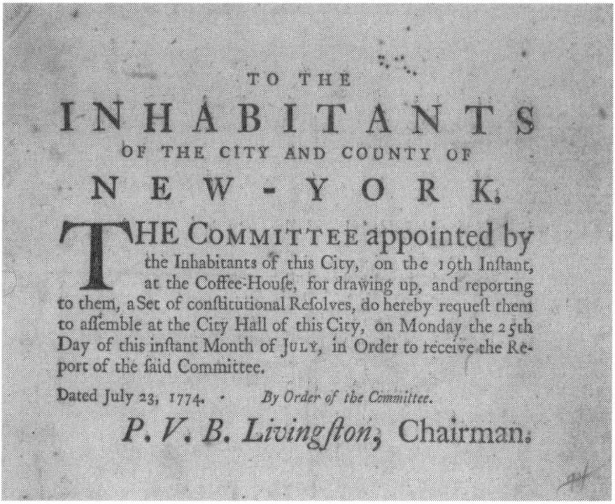

TO THE

INHABITANTS

OF THE CITY AND COUNTY OF

NEW-YORK.

THE COMMITTEE appointed by the Inhabitants of this City, on the 19th Inſtant, at the Coffee-Houſe, for drawing up, and reporting to them, a Set of conſtitutional Reſolves, do hereby requeſt them to aſſemble at the City Hall of this City, on Monday the 25th Day of this inſtant Month of JULY, in Order to receive the Report of the ſaid Committee.

Dated July 23, 1774. *By Order of the Committee.*

P. V. B. Livingſton, Chairman.

FIGURE 2 Flyer for the New-York hyphen debate, 1774.

During his time as Commissioner of Immigration, he penned a famous article that appeared in the recently un-hyphenated *New York Times* entitled, "The Commissioner of Immigration Shows How He Is Hampered." The essay was Curran's response to outrage over the deportation of an immigrant mother who had arrived at Ellis Island with her young children, only to be sent back "home" while her children were to remain in the United States. In the piece, Curran called for the public to afford the judges of such decisions "sympathy more than censure."[2]

Writing in 1924, several years after Roosevelt's speech, Curran accused New York society as being overly judgmental, noting that "it is Ellis Island that catches the devil whenever a decision comes along that does not suit somebody. Of course, we are now in the midst of the open season for attacks on Ellis Island. We have usurped the place of the sea serpent and hay fever. We are ready to be roasted." For the next twelve years he served as Commissioner of Immigration, Curran became more staunchly anti-immigrant, and his hatred was fueled by the anti-hyphenated Americanism espoused by people like Roosevelt and, later, Woodrow Wilson.

Curran was outraged that his beloved city would appear hyphenated, and he continually insisted that Morris call a meeting to pass a law that barred the use of a hyphen in "New York." Meanwhile, curators, historians, and librarians banned together with anti-discrimination and immigrants' rights defenders to defend a hyphenated New-York. Curran could not win this time, they insisted. The curators and librarians at the Historical Society bravely stood by the hyphen in their name, confirming that they had been founded in 1804, that the hyphen was in the original configuration of "New-York," and that, no, this hyphen would not be erased. Hyphenated Americans and activists throughout New York City worried that this erasure would signal that they would not be welcome in the one city that was supposed to be a bastion of openness in America.

In the days leading up to the meeting, head librarian Dorothy Barch proclaimed that despite all of their research, no one had found any documentation indicating that the hyphen in "New-York" had ever been officially deleted by the government or any law-making body in the city, state, or country. The day before the meeting, curator Donald A. Shelley declared that they couldn't even change their name if they wanted to because it is 'chiseled in stone on the front of our building.'"[3]

FIGURE 3 The Hyphen—set in stone.

The press and pressure to enact an anti-hyphenation law were mounting in the lead up to the meeting. Curran insisted that the hyphen was a scourge and that it should be erased completely, as it threatened to divide American society. In erasing the hyphen, Curran wanted to delete hyphenated Americanism altogether. He was firm: the hyphen divides, and as a divider, it threatened the future of the city, the state, the country. As he had done in his role as Commissioner of Immigration, he felt strongly that any immigrant or child of immigrants who identified as anything other than an American should be returned to whatever country was on the other side of that "filthy hyphen."[4] As such, he was emphatic in his attempt to whip the votes of his fellow council members in the lead up to the meeting.

All of this activity garnered a range of emotional reactions. Some people felt that this anger and energy, coming amid the Second World War, was misplaced. The upcoming meeting became the subject of mockery for artists and social commentators alike. At the meeting, a group of musicians and composers performed a song they had written entitled "The Hyphen-Song." The words, written by popular songwriter Leonard Whitcup, included:[5]

> *Take a boy like me, dear*
> *Take the girl I'm dreaming of—*
> *Add a hyphen, what've you got?*
> *You got-UM-M- you've got love!*
> *Me without you-you without me*

It's a sad affair—
But take a tip from the hyphen—
And baby we'll get somewhere

The musicians performed to great acclaim. Activists gathered outside, tying ribbons to the stone etching of the hyphen to highlight the need to protect the orthographic mark that suddenly had so many political and social reverberations.

In the end, much to his chagrin, Curran lost this missive. No law was ever passed outlawing the hyphen, and it remains to this day, etched in stone on the building of the New-York Historical Society, an homage to the journey of the city and the hyphenated individuals who fought the good fight to keep the hyphen—and its many meanings—alive.

Today, the New-York Historical Society hosts hyphen festivals and blogs, and their softball team is named "The Hyphens." Henry Curran died in 1966 at the age of 88. Before his death, and after his hyphen assassination attempt, he went on to be LaGuardia's deputy mayor and the Borough President of Manhattan. He died at Barnabas hospital in New-York.

11 DANI

"Ah, so you must be the roommate," boomed a deep voice. Daniel spun around to lock eyes with a six-foot four blond haired, blue-eyed, bronzed God. When he Googled "Nathan Johnston," the name on the letter announcing his roommate match, the pictures online had not done this man justice.

Daniel bit his lip and nodded slowly. He watched as Nathan's eyes drifted over Daniel's side of the room. His bed was not yet made, and his mis-matched sheets didn't seem long enough for the extra-long twin bed that the liberal arts college dorms favored. He had overstuffed his desk with various papers and knick-knacks that his family had shoved into his bag at the last minute while they rode the bus with him to JFK.

In contrast to Daniel, Nathan's side was exquisitely neat. His bed sheets had been folded down in perfect corners, and his desk was meticulously organized to direct the viewer's attention toward his soccer photographs and trophies.

"So . . . um . . . are you unpacked yet?" Nathan asked, staring at Daniel's desk.

Daniel sighed and jammed his fists into his pockets, "Yep, pretty much. This is me."

"Whoa. Well, um, no offense or anything, man, but I thought you people were supposed to be neat?" Nathan said, not meeting Daniel's eyes. Both men shifted uncomfortably.

Daniel felt a chill run up his spine. He knew that people were constantly stereotyped, but growing up in New York City, it hadn't been much of an issue. Perhaps people silently judged him in his daily life, but no one had been as forward as Nathan was in that moment. And what was he referring to anyway, when he said *you people*? Did he mean Asian-Americans, Chinese-Americans? Or was it because he was gay? And did Nathan even know he was gay?

"Look, um, I didn't mean anything by that. Daniel, is it?" Nathan said. Daniel watched Nathan tuck some unruly locks of curling blond hair behind his ear. Standing in that dorm room, he suddenly felt more uncomfortable than at any other point in his life. He wanted the earth to open up and swallow him whole.

"Actually, it's Dani," he heard himself say. He wasn't sure why he responded that way. He had gone by Daniel his entire life. But something about the move across country, combined with the tidal wave of shame he felt made him want to reinvent himself on the spot.

"Well, Dani. It's good to meet you. And ah, no worries about the mess on your side man, I'm just uh," Nathan cleared his throat. "I'm just glad you don't smell like mothballs or dried fish or anything."

Dani felt another shudder roll down his spine. Did this man truly believe that all Asian-Americans carried dried fish in their pockets? And that all gay people were super neat?

Nathan must have read the confusion on his new roommate's face, because he quickly followed up with, "it's just that my friends in Connecticut had warned me about that."

Dani felt himself flush red and felt the anger rising. He had to get out of that small dorm room, stat. He pushed past Nathan's large body and exited the building as fast as he could.

Outside on Stover Walk, a club fair was going on to attract new students to join any number of student organizations. Like other colleges, Pomona was no exception in that the number of clubs nearly exceeded the number of students—or at least that was how it seemed to Dani. He looked back at his dorm and decided he would rather brave the college fair than return to his problematic roommate.

As he walked down the tree lined, shaded walkway, his eyes caught sight of a small booth decorated by the same red lanterns that lined his mother's kitchen back home. Dani felt himself pulled by the gaggle of dark-haired Asians and Asian-Americans who were smiling and waving at him. He shrugged and drifted toward the group. There were four men and four women hosting the booth. They had a variety of Asian sweets, from Japanese mochi to the mooncakes his mother would make for the Fall festival.

Dani stretched out his hand to introduce himself. He shook hands with the women, who took turns announcing their names (Ming, Christina, Kyoko, and Charlene), then made his way to the men. The first young man, Christopher, sprung back as Dani shook his hand.

"Wait, seriously dude? That's your handshake?" he asked Dani, leaning in closer. "And um, like, no offense or anything, but are you like wearing *guyliner?*" Christopher smirked.

Dani felt himself flush red again. He watched Christopher lean over and whisper something to Christina in Mandarin. She responded while looking Dani up and down, head to toe. "Guess you won't be joining Inter-Varsity then?" she asked. Dani detected a sharp edge in her voice.

Before they could embarrass him any further, Dani shoved his fists into his pockets and made his way down Stover Walk. He didn't look at any of the tables until the very end of the block, where a bright, rainbow-themed booth caught his eye.

Feeling like he didn't have much to lose, he shrugged and made his way over to the booth labelled "Queer Resource Center." In contrast to the many colors of the rainbow behind them, the group of young people were almost entirely white. But they did seem to embody a rainbow of genders, and they welcomed Dani with open arms. Before he knew it, he had signed up to not only be a member of their group, but also to move to their separate dorm as a way to escape his possibly racist, possibly homophobic, possibly both roommate.

"I'm so glad you joined," said Toni, who used they/them pronouns. "I saw you over at the Asian-American booth and didn't think that would go well for you. But don't worry, you'll be super popular here—lots of rice queens, so you'll be in high demand." Dani wasn't sure what to make of the comment but was grateful for the welcome.

"Just one thing: I wouldn't spend much time with the Asian-Americans while you're here, okay sweetheart?" Toni cautioned. "Divided loyalties can be a downfall. You'll have to make sure that we come first," they added, pointing to the rainbow above their head. Dani nodded cautiously.

Toni led Dani to the main orientation hall where Dani sat through one administrator after another welcoming the first-year class to the illustrious Pomona College. After the speechifying had finally finished, students were assigned to small breakout groups—called "Sponsor Groups"—and ordered to various corners of the campus to start to get to know each other and "break the ice." Dani thought that a lot of ice had already been painfully broken.

To his great relief, the leader of his Sponsor Group was one of the people he recognized from the Queer Resource Center booth. They were told to form a circle in a shaded part of the quad.

"Hey everyone, I'm Jade. So, let's start with intros first. Say, um, your name, your PGP, and where you're from, 'kay?"

"Your PGP?" said the woman sitting to Dani's right nervously.

"Preferred gender pronouns," Jade said, matter-of-factly. "Ok, so I'll start. My name is Jade—oh, I guess I already said that—um, I'm from Minnesota, and I use they/them pronouns." Dani noticed Jade winking at him as they made their PGP announcement.

"Ok, I'll go next. I'm Alejandro, I moved here from El Paso, Texas, but I'm originally from Mexico," the man next to Jade said.

"Ahem, and your pronouns?" Jade interjected.

"Oh, um, I use he and him," Alejandro said. He quickly turned to the woman sitting next to him.

"Ok, I'm um Chris, from Connecticut, and I guess I'll say my PGP's but you know there is a lot of research out there saying that people shouldn't be forced to out their pronouns you know? Like it's a lot of pressure. But, um, okay, she/her," Chris said.

"Hi everyone, I'm Helen Ho, she/her/hers pronouns," she said, looking almost sarcastically at Jade. "And I moved here from Berkeley, but I'm originally from Hong Kong—I'm Chinese-American."

It was Dani's turn before he knew it. He had felt the pressure and weight of the opportunity to introduce the new Dani mounting all morning. He took a deep breath before starting.

"Hi everyone, I'm Dani, from New York City," he said, deliberately not adding that he was Chinese-American. "And, um, I use they/them pronouns." Dani was shocked to hear that come out of his/their mouth. But they found that they liked this new identity: Dani, the trans person from NYC. Dani looked up and caught Jade beaming at them, as though they had just announced they were a Nobel Laureate. Helen Ho rolled her eyes and turned her back to Dani, as though to say, "you're a traitor to Chinese-Americans everywhere." There was no room for Chinese-American in the new Dani.

One week later, I heard a soft knock at my office door.

"Come in," I said spinning around in my office chair. I smiled when I saw the shy, young student from my Sexuality and Sexual Politics class the day before. "Hi," I said. "You're, um, Daniel, right?" It always took me a few weeks to learn the names of my new students at the beginning of each semester.

"Um, it's Dani, actually," Dani said. I motioned for Dani to take a seat at my desk.

"I'm so glad you came to office hours, Dani," I said. "It usually takes my male students especially long to come see me."

"Um, actually, I use they/them pronouns," Dani said shyly.

I felt my face flush red. Why was I so bad at this? Why couldn't I get the hang of preferred pronouns? And why had I forgotten, on the first day of class, to have students introduce themselves with them? I would never make that mistake again, I vowed. At that moment I wanted the earth to open and swallow me up.

I breathed hard and apologized. "I'm so sorry, Dani. I won't make that mistake again. And if I do, please call me out on it."

Dani smiled and we both relaxed. "Don't worry about it, Professor. It's actually super new for me. It's something I'm trying out, but it feels really good."

I smiled back. "That's great to hear. And I'm glad you feel safe enough here to try it out."

"It's not all perfect though," they said. "Yesterday I told my mom that I was trans, or maybe transitioning, and she went through the roof."

I nodded, inviting Dani to continue.

"My mom said I was becoming 'too American.' She thinks I'm doing this to shed my Chinese identity. Like there is nothing more American to her than being trans. Do you think she's right?" Dani asked. I could see so much hurt in their eyes at that moment. And I felt such a strong connection to them, recognizing the echoes of my own past and all the years I had tried but failed, leading me to feel guilty about my identity.

"I think you are who you are, Dani," I responded. "And eventually, your mom will see that, and celebrate with you."

Dani stood up, tears in their eyes, and drifted softly out of my office.

12 ANIA 2.0

Ania felt her heart pounding as she walked slowly to the podium at the center of the large room. A group of Indigenous musicians had gathered before the Council of Coalitions meeting that afternoon to play a song to set the stage for the meeting. Each month, the various coalitions rotated who would provide the musical backdrop to the meeting, and, occasionally, various coalitions would bring food and drink.

The Council of Coalitions is ASU's largest and most diverse student governing body, and is technically comprised of seven major groups including The Asian/Asian Pacific American Coalition, The Black African Coalition, the Women's Coalition, The Rainbow Coalition, The Alliance of Indigenous People, The Coalition of International Students, and *El Concilio*, the Latinx students' coalition. These seven coalitions would meet once a month to discuss issues that they had been separately working on and call for collective action.

El Concilio was one of the main reasons Ania had set her sights on ASU. After learning from a friend's older sister about the power of the Latinx group, and after discovering the School of Transborder Studies and School of Social Transformation at ASU, Ania knew she had found her permanent home. From the day she received her acceptance, Ania reached out to students who were members of *El Concilio*, asking how she could join. Now in her sophomore year, Ania had been elected to the executive committee of the group, focusing on student activism. Tonight's meeting to discuss the football team's decision to take part in the nationwide movement to #TakeAKnee was the first time Ania would be addressing the entire council, and she ached with nervousness.

Her passion for activism had not come without a heavy price. After that day in the kitchen, when Ania and her mother fought over Ania's claim to her heritage, she ran away from home, vowing never to return. Her mother had forbidden her from studying anything other than "economics, or something practical," and told her daughter she would be disowned if her mother found out that she was engaging in any kind of political activity.

She had four more weeks until school started and reasoned she could stay at a local shelter until then. After her third night in a women's shelter, Ania decided that it would not be sustainable to remain there. She had been sexually harassed by one of the other women in the middle of the night on her first night there. On the second night, several women gathered to rummage through her belongings, taking what they saw fit. By the third night Ania decided sleep was off the table, so she sat on her bed, eyes wide open, scanning the space for what or whomever would come her way next.

The next day Ania met Brianna, a young woman who looked just a few years older than her. She was a volunteer at the shelter, and took Ania aside to talk with her after noticing how distressed the young woman looked. Brianna told Ania she recognized her from one of the *El Concilio* orientation events that Ania had attended in the Spring. Ania was thrilled to make the connection, but, also embarrassed to be connecting with a future classmate while living as a runaway in a shelter.

Brianna sensed Ania's discomfort almost immediately. "Don't be embarrassed. Why do you think I volunteer here?" Brianna told her new friend. Ania shrugged, tucking a strand of her now filthy hair behind her ear. "I used to *be* you," Brianna added.

Brianna told Ania that she had spent two years in and out of the shelter as a result of an unstable family situation. During one of the periods of time when she left the shelter, she began living on the streets in a small community under the bridge of the 10 and 51 freeways in Phoenix. It was during this time that Brianna learned about Club Fantasy, a popular dungeon in downtown Phoenix.

One of the men under the bridge had watched Brianna put a solicitor in his place one night. Afterwards, this man approached her and told her that Club Fantasy was looking for dominatrixes with "her look," and that they paid good money. Feeling like she had little to lose, Brianna took his advice and went to the club. After just three weeks at Fantasy, Brianna had saved up enough money to rent her own apartment in Phoenix. Six months later, she bought a car.

After two years she was able to save enough to enroll at ASU. She still worked at the club four years later, but Brianna was committed to volunteering at least once a week at the shelter that had been such an important part of her life.

Ania could hardly believe Brianna. Here was this woman who seemed so put together—a beautiful, confident Latina— and all Ania could think was that she wanted to be just like her. The more Brianna talked, the more convinced Ania became that this life—of work at the club, of being self-sufficient—could be the pathway for her. Brianna told Ania that she had the same "look" that the Club Fantasy owners were always looking for. Apparently, their Phoenix customers enjoyed being dominated by Brown women.

"If you're down, we'll leave here tonight, get you all cleaned up, and you can stay with me until you make enough money for your own place, okay?" Brianna said. Ania agreed.

The next day when Ania hesitantly accompanied Brianna to Fantasy, she wondered what her mother would think of this decision. Would she double-disown her? Or would she be pleased that Ania was making money and finally capitalizing on the American Dream?

Ania was offered the job and accepted on the spot. And while at first she lacked the confidence that other women seemed to exude, Brianna was a good teacher, and in a matter of weeks, Ania felt like she was better at her job. A nice side effect was the confidence the job gave her; soon after, she approached the members of *El Concilio* to ask for a leadership position with ease.

The only thing Ania loved more than *El Concilio* meetings were the monthly Council of Coalitions gatherings. She feasted her senses as she watched diverse groups of students pouring into the room, hearing the music of the different coalitions and tasting their rhetorical delicacies. As her eyes drifted across the room, she imagined the stories of different students, wondering how many others were like her, living double, triple, quadruple lives.

Ania steadied herself, waving as her friend Zach walked in. Both students at the SST, Ania and Zach had become good friends—he was almost like an older brother to her. Like Brianna, he was one of the few who knew about her side work. Brianna noticed that Zach was walking in with Ade Ellis, the Sun Devils' new running back. She and Ade locked eyes and nodded at one another. Ania felt desperately jealous at Ade's cool demeanor. He always seemed so comfortable in his own skin, a feeling she had mastered while inside the walls of Club Fantasy, but had yet to conquer in her ASU costume.

I waved to Ania from the back of the room. I had been one of the first professors to welcome her to campus in August, and I felt a strong connection with her. Both she and Zach had invited me to join the Coalition meeting that evening. She caught my eye and smiled; I could tell she was nervous up at the podium.

The music faded out and the groups took their seats in their designated area. Ania tapped the microphone a few times to call people to attention.

"Good evening Coalition members," she began. I watched her grip the sides of the podium to steady herself. "My name is Ania, and I am the head of *El Concilio's* student activism group. We are gathered this evening to talk about coming together in solidarity with hashtag Take A Knee."

The crowd began cheering, whistling, clapping. Ania joined in, clapping from the microphone and pumping her fist into the air. She spoke for a few minutes about her coalition's position and some ideas they had for bringing more attention to #BlackLivesMatter, as well as #TakeAKnee. As her comments drew to a close, I saw two young women from the Black African Coalition raise their hands. Ania gestured to them to speak.

"*Querida,*" one of them began, drawing out the Spanish word for "sweetheart" with sarcastic effect. "*Nosotros tenemos unas preguntas.*"

Ania flinched visibly.

"*Ay dios,*" the other woman jumped in. "*Por que tengo la sensación de que ella no entiende lo que estamos diciendo?*" she asked rhetorically.

I squinted to look at Ania. Could it be that this young woman was correct in her allegation? Did Ania not understand what they were saying? Did she not speak Spanish?

"There you go folks," the first woman said haughtily. "This is your rep? A girl from the suburbs? I bet she is just a rich white girl with a tan."

Ania's face flushed red. "You don't know what you're talking about," she said softly into the microphone.

"Come on girl," the other woman jumped in. "You don't speak Spanish, you aren't a *real* Latina and yet, you're the rep for *El Concilio*? I mean, can you even say the name of your Coalition? I doubt it."

Ania gulped and Brianna joined her onstage. "That's not true, Keisha. She is legit. And I assure you, she is *not* a rich girl from the burbs."

Ania's jaw set tightly and she walked off stage. But the crowd kept going.

"I wanna hear her speak Spanish!" someone called out from *El Concilio's* section.

"Yo, someone check her realness," a voice called out from the Rainbow Coalition.

Zach quickly jumped on stage to reign in the conversation. "Is this why we have gathered tonight, folks? To check other people, to turn on each other? To demand a kind of *realness?*"

The crowd quieted down. "Let's re-focus on the matter at hand," Zach continued.

I followed Ania and Brianna to the back of the room. Four other members of *El Concilio* accompanied them.

"Is it true?" Brianna asked. "Do you really *not* speak Spanish?"

Ania scanned their eyes and avoided mine.

"Look, it's not my fault," she said, feeling as small as she had felt in her mother's kitchen. "My mother. She married a white guy, and then tried to whitewash us. No Spanish allowed."

Brianna nodded sympathetically. But the other members of the group seemed unconvinced.

"I guess that's why you overcompensate then huh? Trying to be all Frida Kahlo and shit. Double major and an expert in Chicana lit? Girl, please," scoffed one of the students.

"Look I hear you girl," interjected another *El Concilio* member. She was attempting a more measured tone, but I could see that Ania was in pain. "But Ania it's like, I don't know. How can you be a real Mexican-American, a *real* Latina if you don't even speak our language? You only speak the language of the colonizers? Talk about divided loyalties. I mean like, who are you?"

The question hung in the air.

PART 3

THE DEATH AND RE-BIRTH OF THE HYPHEN(ATED)

13 HYPHEN THIEF ON-THE-LOOSE?

In the fall of 2007, Angus Stevenson, editor of the *Shorter Oxford English Dictionary* (*SOED*), found himself in the midst of a hyphen mystery that soon became a hyphen controversy. In short, he was accused of murdering a beloved piece of orthography.

"People are not really confident about using hyphens anymore. They're not really sure what they are for," said Stevenson to reporters from *Reuters* to the *New York Times* who were calling him day and night.

In September of 2007, a new edition of the *SOED* was released. And while some of the attendant press surrounding the official launch was on all of the new material—which included 2500 new words and phrases—a not insignificant amount of publicity focused on a tiny piece of connective punctuation that was missing. It turned out that in the 2007 SOED, the hyphen had been removed from some 16,000 words. Many feared the hyphen thieves on the loose—accusing Stevenson of being one such criminal—and called for justice.[1] Stevenson couldn't back down. He had to stand behind his actions. To do so, he sought allies who could help him justify the crime.

Some accomplices blamed technology: "Hyphens are just the latest casualty of the internet age," wrote the Sydney Morning Herald. Geoffrey Leach of Lancaster University told the BBC that electronic communication is partly to blame. "When you are sending e-mails [emails?], and you have to type pretty fast, on the whole it's easier to type without hyphens," Leech said. "Ordinary people are not very conscious of the fact of whether they are putting hyphens or not."

Others blamed the British. "The issue of proper hyphenation has always been vexing for the Brits, far more than it is for us, and occasioned perhaps the single crankiest article in Fowler's *Dictionary of Modern English Usage*, first published in 1926," writes the *New York Times (New-York Times?)*. Henry Watson Fowler, the founder of the *Dictionary of Modern English Usage* noted in reference to the first edition that, "the chaos prevailing among writers or printers or both regarding the use of hyphens is discreditable to English education," About halfway through he threw up his hands and said of the examples he had been citing, "the evidence they afford [is] that common sense is in fact far from common." Fowler was well-known for sprinkling hyphens all over his writing—a distinctly British practice, with other hyphenophiles including Shakespeare (widely cited as the most popular hyphenator ever[2]), Milton, and Donne.

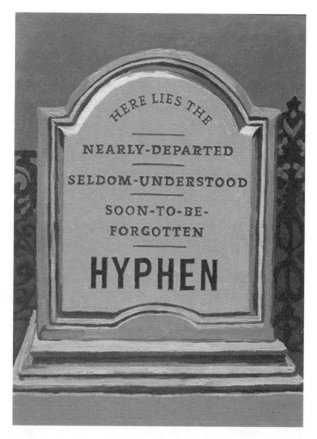

FIGURE 4 Comic response to the new *Shorter Oxford English Dictionary* where numerous hyphens were lost. Image by Ellen Lupton.

The title of a *Reuters* article out of London on the day that the SOED came out in September of 2007 reads "Thousands of hyphens Perish as English Marches On."[3] They were mourning the loss of the hyphen in words like "bumble-bee," which became "bumblebee," "ice-cream," turned "ice cream" and "pot-belly," now "pot belly." "And if you have a problem," Reuters wrote, "don't be such a crybaby (formerly cry-baby)."

Angus Stevenson was not content to stop at citing a decline in usage or levels of confidence from the general public as the main reason for his theft of the precious orthographic mark. Instead of stopping at utility, Stevenson went after the hyphen's physical appearance, citing his distaste for the hyphen's "ungainly horizonal bulk between words."[4]

"Printed writing is very much design-led these days in advert and Web sites," Stevenson said. "And people feel that hyphens mess up the look of a nice bit of typography. The hyphen is seen as messy looking and old-fashioned."

Not surprisingly, Stevenson caused an uproar. Grammarians and activists alike (particularly activists concerned with multicultural issues) were vexed and offended by the hyphen's amputation from the SOED.

Grammarians like Ben Zimmer of Oxford University Press, or Jennifer Buxton and Susan Carter (authors of the popular punctuation guide *Punc Rock: Foundation Stones for Precise Punctuation)* argued that the hyphen, which had stood the test of time since its first invention by Dionysus Thrax, was designed to *connect,* not *divide*. More importantly, they argued, the hyphen joins words and concepts and allows them, over time, to take on new meanings, and new identities.

In *Punc Rock,* Buxon and Carter similarly argued that the writer should have the freedom to choose whether to hyphenate (or not); that this freedom is not a weakness, but rather a strength of this particular punctuation mark. "Hyphens are really tricky," they wrote, "and their usage is constantly changing, so use them with common sense." Later in the book they say that "your eye and your common sense must prevail" and that the hyphen is "a matter of personal fancy." Therefore, they allow lunch break, lunch-break, and lunchbreak, fairy tales, fairy-tales and fairytales. You can take your pick.

Furthermore, Zimmer noted in a blog post on the subject, while "the hyphen has been with us since at least the time of Gutenberg, and over time certain general rules have developed, none of the rules are hard and fast."[5]

Writing in response to the new SOED, Zimmer wrote that "as modern English has evolved, some compounds have stayed 'open' as two words separated by a space (*snow tire, fire hose, water cooler*), while many others have become 'closed' with no intervening space or hyphen (*snowman, fireplace, watermelon*). The hyphenated version is very often a way-station (way station? waystation?) between an open compound and a closed compound, as the form becomes more entrenched in written usage (*hand writing* becomes *hand-writing* becomes *handwriting*)."[6]

Thus the power of the hyphen itself absolutely cannot be underestimated. As the language has evolved, it has been this small piece of orthography that has created new words, imbued them with new meanings, and allowed us to speak and write in new ways, even as society transforms. Indeed, the political and grammatical pressure behind the vanishing hyphens—and the grammatical mark's resistance to vanishing—highlight the power that lives inside the hyphen itself.

The hyphen has the power to make two become one. Two compound words may start as health care, and then move to health-care, and finally graduate to healthcare. That the hyphen drops out is not a testament to its weakness—quite the contrary, say grammarians like Sarah Townsend. In an article on how to use compound words, she explains that "many words that begin as hyphenated compounds become so commonplace that the hyphen ends up being dropped—it's a natural part of the evolution of the English language."

For Stevenson's part, he was surprised at the hyphen controversy that followed him. Letters such as the two below were published in the *New York Times,* and hundreds of blogs defending the power of the hyphen followed.

Oct. 12, 2007

To the Editor:

Re "Death-Knell. Or Death Knell" (Week in Review, Oct. 7):

Without consultation, the editor of the Shorter English Dictionary, Angus Stevenson, is diminishing the role of the hyphen. I object vehemently! I am a hyphenator! To use the hyphen is to clarify. The hyphen makes the word easier to read. I shall not be constrained in its use by the Shorter English Dictionary renegades!

Why is the hyphen being moved out of its well-regarded position among writers of the English word? Is it being demoted to an inferior role in order to save space on the page? Has the green movement gone mad?

Oxford editors, roll back the hyphen ruling! I proclaim my refusal to concede this usage change! As a writer of the English word, I shall continue to hyphenate whenever I can! Dashed if I won't!

Robert Niner

Longwood, Fla., Oct. 7, 2007

To the Editor:

Re "Death-Knell. Or Death Knell," about the Oxford English Dictionary's removal of hyphens from many words because people are "not really sure what they're for":

I added a hyphen to my first name at the suggestion of my high school guidance counselor when I started applying to colleges.

My first name looks like two names. I don't have a middle name or initial, and I hate being called Mary because that's not my name.

My late husband thought it was so amusing that one of his pet names for me was Hyphen. So it's a bit disconcerting to find out, thanks to your article, that I'm "probably an affectation."

Oh puh-leez!

Mary-Ellen Banashek
New York, Oct. 9, 2007

Stevenson remained defensive—angry, even—that so many hyphenophiles were leveling accusations from theft to murder against him. At one point he even went so far as to state that he was only reflecting a societal trend, and that society had stopped hyphenating because "people did not want to reach for the hyphen key on a computer." This was the last straw. The full force of hyphen protectors would be unleashed, as the orthographic marker would become a moral turning point. It was a time when the majority started to fight back, arguing for the power and importance of the hyphen in society.

Stevenson's SOED set off a powerful conversation that—like the hyphen itself—brought together people who wanted to defend the notion of hyphenated Americanism with grammarians, literature lovers, and Shakespeareans. It inadvertently started a conversation about the power that lives inside the hyphen itself, and, in turn, allowed hyphenated individuals and hyphen-lovers the chance to assert that power, their power, on their own terms.

14 THE BIG MOMENT

It was the summer of 2007. I was nervous, as nervous as I had ever been. As dozens of people streamed into the University of Tehran lecture hall, I consciously slowed my breathing to calm myself. Then, I felt a hand on my shoulder.

It took me a moment to realize it was my friend Raya, cloaked in black. She usually wore vibrant colors and a broad, mischievous smile. Today her expression was muted; the only color I saw was from one lock of red highlighted hair, deliberately pulled out from her black head scarf. "I just wanted to wish you good luck," she said with a wink and a hint of a smile that belied our shared nervousness. Raya moved silently to find a seat at the back of the room, close to the doors, always ready for an escape.

I was there to talk about sexual politics in Iran, which I had been studying for the previous seven years. Since 9/11, I had dedicated myself to studying Iranian feminism, reasoning that I was clearly more Iranian than American. But when I arrived in Iran to begin my fieldwork, I was constantly reminded that just as I was too Iranian in America, I was too American in Iran. In Tehran, my constantly slipping headscarf combined with how I carried myself—shoulders back, eyes ablaze—revealed that I wasn't raised in the Middle East. Beyond my comportment, young Iranians ridiculed my "kitchen Farsi" and made fun of my accent when I spoke. I was ashamed of my weak linguistic skills (up until then I thought my Farsi was excellent!), and even more embarrassed at my lack of Islamic fashion sense.

Raya was one of the inspiring women who was not only a compelling research subject, but also rekindled my own belief in an Iranian feminist identity; she and other women helped strengthen my sense of belonging when I felt lost back "home" in the US.

I knew presenting at the University of Tehran was risky, but Raya and her friends had convinced me it was important for the integrity of my work that I reveal the results publicly in Iran before the book was published in the US. I knew this was a high-stakes endeavor: any possible critique of the regime could be genuinely life threatening. I had already seen too many women carted off to Evin, Iran's most notorious prison. But I also knew it was time to stand behind the research and writing I had gathered about Iran's sexual revolution, and behind the women whose movement I was documenting.

The waiting felt interminable. My stomach churning, I could barely hear the head of the social sciences department finally introduce me. But then, applause. I headed to the front, up five stairs to the stage.

I gripped the podium with one hand to steady myself and opened the navy-blue folder that held my lecture notes.

Deep breath. I started, as I often do, by describing a gathering of young women talking about their sexualities as politics. I began laying out my theory that sexual revolutions give birth to social movements. As I looked up and scanned the audience, I spotted Raya again, seated on the left side of the center section, about 20 rows back.

I kept talking, feeling my nerves calm, my voice more steady. And then, exactly 14 minutes after I began, all six sets of the auditorium doors banged open at once. I stopped mid-sentence.

I cannot remember if I first saw, smelled, or heard them. Boots stomped and men rushed in, reeking of cigarettes. They had no reverence for the place or any care for the people gathered there. Chains clanked and weapons bumped the armrests of chairs as they stormed past. The professor who had introduced me stood and ran to one of them, but he was shoved aside. A few audience members tried to intervene, but most people ran for the exits.

It was chaos, and I was frozen, gripping the podium and my lecture notes—which I should have been shredding. I watched what was happening as if it were in slow motion, all the while desperately searching for Raya, until I found her near the back of the room.

One of the guards was grabbing her by her neck. I knew they would be taking her to Evin, where she would likely be held in solitary confinement for days, months, possibly even years. I wanted to scream, but I knew to keep it inside. Then I heard only a ringing in my ears as the auditorium erupted with everyone screaming, while still no sound came from my throat.

Pandemonium continued, yet four guards made their way through the crowd and jumped onto the stage—no need for stairs. They yanked me by the arms and pulled me off the stage. I knew better than to fight back. One of them kicked my shins, causing me to buckle to the floor. That's when I heard a whoosh and turned my head to look up.

Everything went black.

It turned out that I was one of the lucky ones. I wasn't taken to Evin—I hadn't warranted a spot there, one of the Revolutionary Guards told me. I was taken back to my apartment which by then had been ransacked and emptied of most of my belongings. I was told to remain there, indefinitely.

Each day I wondered if I would be taken to Evin or if I would be disposed of, taken out to the hills outside Tehran, my body left for dead. I was accused of being a spy for the US, while also combatting accusations of running a prostitution ring and trying to foment a velvet revolution.

I'm a scholar, I told them repeatedly. I'm on a quest to understand where I fit into this world, I confessed to myself. My journey toward self-discovery, my newly rekindled love affair with feminism, and my desire to do something for my home country had come at a high price.

But I have just started fitting somewhere, I sobbed one day to my interrogator, broken by the emotional torture. I have finally found home, I gulped. "This is not your country, *khawhar,*"[1] my interrogator barked. "You are a traitor to this country and you will never call Iran home."

I didn't know what my interrogator's name was, but I had taken to calling him Sumac in my head because he always returned from his mercifully long lunch breaks with flecks of the blood red spice wedged between his teeth.

For the first two days, no one set foot inside my apartment. I was thrown inside, told I could not leave, shown the guard outside the apartment who would ensure my obedience, and then left to my own devices. I alternately cried, vomited until there was nothing left, and slept. On the third day, Sumac arrived, announcing his presence by slamming the front door and screaming *"Khawhar! Hejabet ra rahayat kon!"* (Sister, guard your veil). I wanted to respond with, "brother guard your eyes," the usual feminist clapback, but I held my tongue.

And then the questioning began. Sumac was especially loquacious, and would often answer the firing squad of his questions with his own hypotheses of the answers. "Are you helping the *Amricayees* foment a revolution? Of course you are because all you Americans want to come together to use feminism to bring down this Islamic Republic. Did you start a prostitution ring? Of course you did because you're a prostitute, too. Did you like hanging out with prostitutes? Yes, because you fit right at home with them. Did you lie to the Minister about your 'research'? That's obvious, because you're a woman, and you all lie." On and on he would go.

I quickly discovered that his diarrhea of the mouth was useful. In listening to his questions and subsequent hypotheses, I pieced together what the charges were against me, and who or what might have landed me in this mess. Sumac would come each morning around 7 a.m., leave at noon for a long lunch, then return for another five-hour round of questioning. This happened every day except for Friday; that was how I marked the passage of time when my mind played tricks on me and I lost count of the hours or days.

"Why are you here?" barked Sumac, his usual opening question. "Because I love my country," I responded obediently, my usual response. Sentences and memories would flood my brain each time I tried to sleep. I came in search of my true Iranian identity and realized I didn't fit in anywhere. I would flutter my eyes open, wanting to write a thought, an idea, a response. *If only I had my notebook, a pen, some paper, something,* I thought. At one point I started using the bottom of my gray—God knows how old—toothbrush, one of the very few things I was permitted to have, to etch out writings on the wood floor beneath my bed. At first, I had only pretended to write, using the floor as paper, the toothbrush as an invisible pen. Holding its rectangular column between my fingers had felt unnatural, though the act of writing put me at ease.

"It's not your country, sister," Sumac growled. "Iran is for believers, not traitors like you." His usual response. In the early days of questioning I had avoided his gaze, preferring to look down at the dented plastic table they had installed in my apartment for questioning. While looking down I would see the width of Sumac's thighs spilling over the plastic chair he sat in. When he stood up, Sumac took up what seemed like half of the room. He was tall, taller than most Iranian men I knew, towering at about 6'4, or so it seemed. His army green uniform pants were too short for him, revealing mismatched socks on most days. And the rolls of fat that poured over the top of his pants were barely contained by the green and yellow jacket he wore each day, despite the sweltering heat. The guards who took turns stationed outside my door usually removed their outercoats and hats, but Sumac rarely did, preferring the constraint of the polyester fabric that tried to contain his guts.

One time, during an especially long and heated questioning session, as Sumac asked for the details of a group sex party, he became more flushed than usual and removed his jacket, unbuttoning his collar as he read out the details from one of my recently published articles. It was then that I saw that the thin linen fabric of his shirt was no match for the sheer force not only of Sumac's flesh, but also the thick coarse forest of black hairs that sprung out of every pore in his body, barely tamed on his face, and dense enough to make his shirt hover an inch above his shoulders. The hair on his head was equally unruly, reigned in on certain days by what seemed like an entire bottle of hair gel that, when mixed with his sweat, produced a nauseating smell of something like chemically infused onions.

"How can you call yourself Iranian? Have you no shame? You dishonor this country. Write lies that you sell to those

Amricayees—your *real* country—and make a fortune out of helping those filthy heathens to feel good about feeling bad when they think of us," Sumac spat. At first I found these accusations ridiculous, unjust, and unfair, but over time, I started to realize that I wasn't on one side of the hyphen or the other. Rather, my power, my authority, my authenticity came from *inside* the hyphen itself. What was my identity? I was a hyphenated feminist activist. And my many selves were powerful—so powerful that they threatened an entire country's social and political security.

Still, this journey was not easy. I realized through my interrogation that feminism, activism and bridging (and setting) the terms of hyphenated identities including my own *was* my identity. This work gave my life meaning. Like so many young people I met in Iran and in the US, I, too, was an activist in a movement where we used our bodies to resist power, to attack the fabric of morality woven by the regime.

On certain days, I wondered if I had lost or found my sense of self. Was I, as Sumac suggested, betraying my country and religion by being a woman, and Iranian-American, and an activist, all at the same time? Or was Sumac just getting into my head? This was always the worst part for everyone who had spent time being held captive by the Revolutionary Guards—when we couldn't figure out what our brains were really thinking.

Over the next few weeks I was overtaken with insomnia. At night, exhausted from a long day of questioning, I would lie awake in bed, fighting my demons. I thought about Sumac's questioning and how in his awfulness, he had opened doors for me to think in a new way. But, I wondered, had I shamed my Iranian ancestors by being woman and feminist? Did the activist in me need to be exorcised before I could be a true, good Iranian woman? These questions swirled in my mind night after night until one night I fell into a deep sleep. That night I dreamt that I was locked in a jail cell in Evin with four versions of me—all of whom were criticizing me. In the dream, I brought the many me's together, realizing that we could keep doing battle, or we could be four times stronger by coming together in one body. I awoke as my selves fused inside me.

Thirteen days later, I was kicked out of my ancestral home country, stripped of my Iranian citizenship, and told never to return. Never again could I be where my search for myself had landed me.

It took getting arrested and kicked out of Iran to wrap my limbs around the hyphen. But, once I did, I found the power inside.

15 THE BIG GAME

Ade hadn't slept well in days. Ever since the day of the interview with the reporter whom he had shunned, and, more importantly, ever since the Council of Coalitions meeting, Ade found himself unable to sleep, his mind filled with questions and scenarios.

The members of the Black African Coalition had come to him, begging him to join them. And his conversations with Zach and his professors in the African and African-American Studies (AAAS) Department had inspired him to start reading more about the history of African and African-American thought. He was now reading everything from Malcom X to Frantz Fanon, steeped in the literature.

His fellow players on the football team took notice, as did the coaches. While the coaches kept telling him to "get his head in the game," his fellow players found his appetite for Black literature inspiring.

"It's about time, brother," Darius had said when he found Ade reading Ta-Nehisi Coates' *Between The World And Me*.

"It's hard for me to reconcile Brother West and Brother Coates' different takes on reparations," Ade confessed to

Darius, referring to Cornel West, a philosopher and activist whose work Ade had been reading recently.

"You'll get there, Ade, you will," Darius had responded. "But just get there fast. We're gonna need you to kneel at the big game ok?"

Ade still hadn't made up his mind about whether or not he would, in fact, be taking a knee during the national anthem. It was true that Colin Kaepernick, who had started the trend back in 2015, was his idol. But it was also true that Kap had paid dearly for his decision to do so: he hadn't played professional football since. To lose his only true family in the world—his fellow players—seemed too high a price to pay.

Or was it? After all, wasn't Kap only doing what was right, kneeling to make a statement about African-Americans and the sordid history of the US? And how many friends would he lose by *not* kneeling?

The night before the game, Zach had invited Ania—the troubled young woman who was publicly humiliated by the Council that night that was etched in Ade's brain—and a few other friends to their dorm room. They had a lengthy discussion about capitalism, identity, and the need to use their bodies to speak truth to power. Ade recalled feeling in that moment like he belonged more in that dorm room, with all these other individuals who lived in the in-between, than at any other point or place in his life. He listened as Zach announced that he had many identities—rural-American, gay-American, Christian-American, and activist among them—and that he could embrace his many identities rather than see them as competing or hostile to one another.

"Other people don't get to define us," Zach said. "We who live in what Dr. Mahdavi calls the 'in-between' we define those terms, and defining ourselves on our own terms—that gives us power."

Ade had mulled over Zach's words all night.

Now the morning of the Big Game had arrived. Ade was tired and his body ached all over. He felt a jolt as his phone buzzed next to him; Ade saw his father's name and almost didn't answer. But at the last moment, he changed his mind.

"'Sup, Ellis?" Ade answered. He had taken to calling his father by his last name since their drive from Texas to Arizona. It felt appropriately formal and distant. And he could never get his lips to form the word "dad."

"Listen Ade, you listen to me now, you hear?" his father commanded.

"It's Ade*Chike*, Ellis, you know that," he shot back.

"Ade, cut the crap. I don't have time for this. Listen to me, son," he said. Ade flinched. His father kept going. "You best not be thinking of kneeling tonight, you hear? You take a knee, your life is over. Don't try to be a hero."

AdeChike turned his father's words over. "I'm not a hero. That's all you, Ellis," AdeChike said sarcastically. He knew his father loved thinking of himself as a war hero, and AdeChike always felt uncomfortable with the fact that his father identified as a veteran before anything else.

"I'm serious, Ade. Don't try to be like Kap, or Darius, or anyone else who fills your head with crap at that school, you hear me?" his father boomed. "You're an American. You're my son. And no son of mine will disrespect our country by kneeling during the anthem. For Christ's sake, your father is a veteran. Please tell me you aren't even considering this?"

"Gotta go Ellis, gotta get ready," AdeChike said and hung up the phone. He felt beads of sweat form in the tight curls at his temples.

Darius and two other guys stopped by his dorm room to walk over to the stadium together. AdeChike thought it lucky they had come; his instinct had been to blow off the game altogether. But then he remembered Coach Carl, back in Texas, saying that the he was the leader, the glue that kept the team together. He couldn't let his team down. What did that mean tonight? Could he let his people down for the sake of his team? Could he turn a blind eye to centuries of abuse and violence against his ancestors? Could he just erase the part of him that was as much African as American, like his father had? Could he erase his mother's memory?

These questions plagued him as they walked into Sun Devil Stadium. As the players gathered, AdeChike told Darius to tell the coaches he would be down in the locker room momentarily, he just had to make a quick stop. Darius looked at him, concerned, but agreed.

AdeChike ran up the stands, taking the steps three or four at a time until he reached the main sound booth. He ran right inside to find the production team.

"Hey Ade, what are you doing here?" one of the young men asked in surprise.

"I need a favor," AdeChike said.

Ten minutes later he ran back down to the locker room, careful not to trip over the stairs as he hurried back. The other players were gathering and there was a buzz of nervous energy in the air. AdeChike knew that he wasn't the only one wrestling with his decision that night.

Before the coaches came in Darius called a group of the Black players together out in the hallway.

"Let's not lose focus, brothers. We do what we came to do. We stand in solidarity with our brothers across the country," Darius said.

"And with Kap!" said another voice.

"And with Black Lives Matter!" came another voice.

Fists pumped into the air, and AdeChike felt his heart pounding.

It was time for the game to start. He could hear the fans pouring into Sun Devil Stadium. And as he saw the ASU Mascot, Sparky, wander by, he knew it was time for them to make their big entrance.

This used to be AdeChike's favorite part, when the players were introduced on the jumbo screen and they burst through balloons, or paper, or throngs of fans onto the field as soon as their name was called. He heard Darius' name and watched him bounce through waving his hands to pump up the crowd. He was next.

"Neeeext up, your star, number thirty three . . . ." The announcer over enunciated each word. "AAaaaaade*Chike* Oyubango Ellis!!"

AdeChike could almost hear his father gasp. And he looked out onto the field to see several of his teammates looking up at the screen in confusion. His usual introduction was "Ade Ellis," but he called in a favor with the media team and changed it at the last minute.

Rather than jumping up and down, AdeChike walked calmly through the crowd then took his place on the field. He made his right hand into a fist, bumped his heart and then pointed to the sky.

"He's thinking about his mom," Zach leaned over and whispered to me. I nodded in agreement.

The players all took the field one by one. Then the introductions were over and it was time for the national anthem.

"Laaaadies and gentlemen, please stand for America's national anthem, sung by one of our very own students, Kailey Mitchell!" the announcer boomed.

"If it's only ladies and gentlemen then maybe I don't need to stand?" Zach joked nervously. We both stood staring at the field, wondering what would happen next.

Kailey went to the microphone and began her acapella version of the anthem. Everything seemed to be moving in slow motion.

Several players, led by Darius and Jackson, removed their helmets and kneeled on the grass. I watched AdeChike in suspended animation.

He slowly removed his helmet. Then, eyes to the sky, he sank down and took a knee. The crowd went wild.

No one would remember who won the game that night, all anyone could talk about were the ASU Sun Devils who took a knee. After the game reporters rushed to AdeChike for comment.

"So Ade, tell us, what made you take a knee?" one reporter asked. Others echoed the question.

"First, it's Ade*Chike,* that's my full name," he said smiling. "But, more important, I took a knee for me, and for my ancestors. I took a knee to honor my many selves" The crowd went wild again.

16 THE BIG DEBATE

"To hyphenate or not to hyphenate? That is the question at hand, folks," announced Josh, proud member of the self-titled Nerd Squad who congregated every Friday for lunch on the quad of Google Inc's main campus.

The marine layer had largely burned off (why Googlers insisted that there was a "marine layer" this far inland, in Mountainview, was beyond me), but it was still chilly by noon on a Friday in July of 2012. I spent most of that summer at the Silicon Valley campus, known as the "mothership" to insiders, in Northern California. I often felt out of place there, like I had lost my way. But lately, more people on campus were recognizing me, and inviting me to join events and conversations.

I was the odd woman out, I felt, in a sea of people who prided themselves on their oddness. A long-time academic, I had taken up a position at Google Ideas, the "think/do tank" arm of Google Inc. They had recently decided—like many other tech firms wanting to join the wave of corporate social responsibility in "innovative" ways—that they wanted to use their technology to "disrupt illicit networks." They fixated on human trafficking, convinced that there was a connection between human trafficking and terrorism. They had hired me to help their coders figure out how to "disrupt" such networks, and thus save the world.

At lunch I would collect my food in the cafeteria and sometimes sit alone at a booth, eavesdropping on conversations about building the first self-driving car or Google X, the mystery tech that Astro Tellar was developing. While Google's campus was somewhat diverse in terms of ethnic background, gender diversity was not quite on par. In other words, as a female in my thirties, I was a somewhat rare commodity. As Google Ideas surrounded itself with more and more mystique, I became a person of interest; this was how I landed myself a standing invitation to the Nerd Squad.

When I carried my tray over to join the group of mostly male Googlers, they were already in the midst of a fairly heated debate. Apparently one of the coders was trying to argue in favor of doing away with nonbreaking (nonbreaking? non breaking?) hyphens, reasoning that their code was too clunky. Others resisted, pointing out that nonbreaking hyphens were an absolute necessity.

"Imagine writing I-5 or I-405 without the hyphen," said Vivek, an Indian-American coder who had moved to Silicon Valley earlier that year from Google's Austin campus. "I mean, California—and Californians—are defined by these freeways. How are you gonna take that out of the code?"

"Or how about your phone number?" said James, a Korean-American graphic designer who had just graduated from Stanford. "How would you do a phone number without nonbreaking hyphens?"

"I'm not saying take the dashes out assholes," said Philip, who identified as white and American. He grew up in San Diego, but had been living in Northern California since he moved up north to attend college at the age of 16. "I'm saying we don't need to have a whole U+2011 code for 'nonbreaking hyphens.' They seem useless. Ugly, even."

As I so often found myself doing around the Nerds, I pulled out my Google Android and began Googling away. I of course knew the difference between a hyphen and a dash— and I sensed the power of the hyphen was understated. But what exactly was the difference between nonbreaking and other hyphens?

A quick Google search revealed the answer. I tried to take in all the HTML coding language as rapidly and discreetly as possible. The debate was shaping up in an interesting way; I watched the Chinese-Americans, Korean-Americans, Japanese-Americans, Indian-Americans and Pakistani-Americans drift to one side of the table, leaving the White males on the other. I wanted to keep scanning the physical space and pulsing for the tension, but I had to figure out what exactly they were all talking about.

I went back to my Google search. Oddly enough, it was my employer's rival, Microsoft, who had the best description for what a non-breaking hyphen actually is. According to their "help" page:

You can often improve the look of your document by keeping certain words and paragraphs together on the page or across page breaks. Also, you can use hyphenation to improve overall readability. Keep words on the same line with a nonbreaking hyphen. Word automatically breaks the text at a space or a hyphen at the end of a line. To keep two words or a hyphenated word together on one line, you can use a nonbreaking space or nonbreaking hyphen instead of a regular space or hyphen.[1]

Another popular grammarian blog, WordTips went on to say this of the nonbreaking hyphen:

When Word calculates line length and wraps text to the next line, it tries to break the line at a space or a hyphen—a dash. Sometimes, however, you may not want Word to break a line at a dash. For instance, dashes are used in telephone numbers, and you might not want a line to break in the middle of a telephone number.

The answer to this dilemma is to use non-breaking hyphens instead of regular dashes when you don't want Word to break a line at the hyphen. To do this, hold down the **Ctrl** and **Shift** keys as you type the dash (this is the same as typing **Ctrl** and an underscore). Word will then not break the line at that point.[2]

Josh and Philip's argument was that the code for a non-breaking hyphen was too onerous. They felt that the writer had to go through too many steps when using, for example, the lowly software Microsoft Word, to make a nonbreaking hyphen happen. For that reason, they argued, nonbreaking hyphens—and hyphens altogether—should just get out of the way to make room for dashes.

"You don't get it," said Vivek. "Just because something is onerous doesn't mean it's not useful, necessary, and beautiful."

"You sound like you're talking about your self-driving car, Viv," Josh retorted.

"I feel like you really don't get it, though," said Suresh, a Pakistani-American coder from Boston. "The dash isn't the same as the hyphen. The dash divides. The hyphen connects. Brings together."

"I feel like you're taking it personally," said Jonathan, a white designer from Florida.

"I feel like he should take it personally. And it is political," said James. "It's political for a lot of us."

"Look, you might not know this, but there was a lot of controversy around the hyphen like less than a hundred years ago," said Tim, a Chinese-American coder. "When my great grandparents moved to the U.S., the term 'hyphenated American' was a derogatory term they used against Asian immigrants here. And it came back during World Wars I and II to question divided loyalties."

"Seriously?" said Josh. He looked from James to Tim to Vivek and then back to his team of Nerds which included Jonathan, Philip and a handful of others.

"The hyphen isn't just grammar, it's politics. It's history," James added. "And you'll have to forgive us if we, as Asian-Americans, seem defensive towards people like you wanting to erase it."

"People like us?" Philip challenged.

"Guys, chill. We're trying to give you context behind the code. Isn't that what sets Googlers apart from others—we understand context?" Vivek jumped in to diffuse the tension.

"Plus, why would you want to take such an elegant piece of code and dump it?" Suresh said. "Nonbreaking hyphens are powerful. They keep things together that need to be kept together. Would you really do away with that if you could?"

Josh and Jonathan looked at each other and there was silence for a while.

"And I guess that in some ways all Americans could be hyphenated right?" Josh said cautiously after almost a minute had passed. "Like, I could say I'm Jewish-American?"

"You're totally hyphenated, bro," said Vivek.

"Hyphens can be powerful. Look at this code for a nonbreaking hyphen: a piece of punctuation that holds more power than a letter, that physically brings things, people, places together," said Tim.

"Right. It's like, hyphens—does it get any better than that?" James added.

"To hyphens then," said Josh raising his can of Diet Coke. "To hyphenating, and to the hyphenated."

17 THE BIG READ

Ania sighed as she lifted her heavy bag of props and costume equipment out of the tiny trunk of the Smart Car she purchased last month. It was her fourth night in a row at Club Fantasy, and the ache in her bones combined with the general sense of heaviness she felt made her realize why most of the girls never worked more than two nights in a row.

Ever since the incident at the Council of Coalitions, Ania had been spending most of her free time at the Club. She was avoiding El Concilio members, and had stopped attending social events altogether. The Club, she told herself, was where she had the power, where she didn't have to be worried about being judged, where *she* was doing the judging.

At first this power had been intoxicating. But then as she picked up more shifts, she felt more confused, emptier. Before this point she reasoned that the Club was a side hustle; it was something that made her extra money to always have a soft landing pad, to have security in her choice to never go back to her family for help. And the gig was lucrative, she told herself. She had saved enough to purchase a small car—her first!—and many of her clients showered her with expensive gifts that made her feel important.

But if she was being honest with herself, she missed school, and she missed El Concilio. Lately, she hadn't even been attending classes. It was all she could do to attend the Big Game against the University of Arizona, and she did that more out of a sense of curiosity about her new friend, AdeChike. She felt pride watching him take a knee. But that was the last time she had felt real joy, she realized.

As she dressed in the dungeon locker room, she felt a hand on her shoulder. She turned to see Brianna, a worried look on her face.

"You're here again, Ni?" Brianna said. Her voice was stern, though she used the nickname that only Ania's brothers had used growing up. Whenever she heard this version of her name, her heart tightened with grief.

"Leave me alone, Bri. I'm making good money," Ania shot back. She turned back to her bag, rummaging for her whips.

"We both know this isn't about money, Ni," Brianna said, softly this time.

Ania wouldn't face her friend. She kept her attention focused on getting dressed and finding the right tools for her client that evening. Brianna wrenched Ania's bag from her hand and threw it to the floor. Ania was taken aback. She knew that this was how Brianna performed in the dungeon— even she performed this way, sometimes—but she had never seen Brianna try a power move on her. She was so shaken that she slumped to the floor and grabbed her knees. Brianna realized she had moved too fast, exerted too much power.

"I'm sorry Ni," Brianna said softly. She sank to the floor to put an arm around her friend. Ania slowly felt herself curling into a ball. She bit her lip to fight back the tears that had been building up for months.

"Look, you know I'm not judging you, right?" Brianna continued. "It's just that, well, this isn't *you*."

"What do you mean?" Ania asked.

"Come on *mija,* you and I both know that the Club isn't really *you* the way it is me," Brianna said. Ania flinched.

"What? Like I'm not good enough?" Ania said defensively.

"That's not it, and you know it's not. Come on Ni, put your guard down, it's just me."

Both women were silent for a time, then Ania broke the silence. "I'm not sure I understand what you are trying to say."

"Listen, hear me out. And try not to get defensive for once, alright?" Brianna said. Ania nodded slowly.

"It's not that you aren't good at the job here. What I mean is that this isn't what fuels you the way it fuels me. And look, that's not a bad thing," Brianna continued. "I've seen you at rallies and El Concilio meetings. That look you get in your eye? That's the look I get when I'm here at the Club. But for you—your power comes at school. And, if I'm being honest, I kind of envy that."

Ania felt the tears coming fast now and she thought about that scene in *Like Water for Chocolate* again. She didn't try to fight them this time.

"Don't cry, Ni," Brianna said quickly. "This is a good thing. You, your power comes from leading, from a passion to change the world. And you are going to. But you can't lose your way. And the more time you spend here at the Club, the more lost you are going to feel. You need to get back to campus. Get back to those books that only you can make sense of. Let me take it from here with the Club. You go change the world, okay?"

Ania felt like her tears were flooding the locker room. She wasn't sure if they were tears of joy, relief, anger, or sadness; but just like she was a combination of so many selves, so too were her tears a cocktail that came of all her mixed emotions.

She went back to the dorms that night and dove back into her schoolwork. She began reading with a fierce appetite, like someone who had been dieting for weeks and was just now breaking their fast. She felt transformed by her readings, from transnational feminist theory to Chicana literature.

The next week, after her brief hiatus, she came back to Trans Fem. I happened to be speaking in class that week and hugged Ania as I walked in. She seemed like a different person than the hurt young woman I had seen crawl off the stage at the Council of Coalitions meeting a few months earlier. I watched her take a seat next to Zach, who put his arm reassuringly around her.

"How's AdeChike?" I heard her ask Zach as the other students filed in.

"He's fighting his own demons, but coming out stronger too," Zach responded. The two of them exchanged smiles.

Five minutes past the hour, class began. We talked about the importance of self-reflection and understanding your position as a feminist. I was introducing the twin concepts of reflexivity and positionality, and had asked the students to read *A Thrice Told Tale* by Margery Wolf, the post-modernist (postmodernist? Post modernist?) feminist theorist. The book is a cautionary tale of what can happen when feminist researchers are not reflective of their position, their power, and their privilege with regards to the people they study.

"What, so does this mean that as a white woman I can never do research in communities of color because I can never be reflexive enough?" said one student who had introduced herself as Miriam.

"I don't think that's what it means," Zach jumped in. "I think it means that we have to draw on our different selves to make bridges, and be cognizant of our position."

"That doesn't make sense," Miriam shot back. "Are you talking about code switching?"

"Always with the code switching," said Shanna, a student I recognized from her leadership of the Black African Coalition on campus.

"I think it's more about self-reflection and bridging than code-switching," Ania ventured. I could see that she was worried about speaking up and that part of her was afraid she would be critiqued, but she clearly had something to say. I encouraged her to continue.

"It's just like Gloria Anzaldua says in *This Bridge Called My Back*. Some of us are really good at bridging because, well, we've always *been* a bridge. Like, I feel like my body is a bridge, and my whole life has been a bridge. But I've always been so focused on where I was bridging *to* or bridging *from*. Now I realize I can focus on the bridge itself," Ania said.

Other students snapped their fingers and nodded their heads.

"Preach," said Shanna appreciatively. Ania looked around and a big smile came across her face. I watched her audibly exhale.

"What was that book called you just mentioned?" Miriam asked Ania. I watched Ania lean over into her backpack.

"It's an anthology called *This Bridge Called My Back*," I said. Ania fished her copy of the book out of her bag, proudly showing it to the class. The book had been marked up, tagged and flagged; it looked like my most cherished readings.

"This Bridge, I mean this book, has been changing my life," Ania said. "It was like meeting Gloria Anzaldua, who struggles with being neither here nor there and finally embraces the in-between, allowed me to finally appreciate living inside a bridge."

"Or a hyphen," I added. "I've been embracing life inside the hyphen, myself." Ania and Zach both nodded emphatically.

When class was over, Zach and Ania lingered in the classroom, talking as I gathered up my things.

"Looks like you've been slaying some demons too—and I'm not talking about your slaying in the dungeon," Zach said to his friend.

"I quit the Club," Ania said proudly. Zach raised his eyebrows in surprise.

"It's just not *me*," she announced to him, winking as she caught my eye. She had told me her story a week before, and we had been emailing back and forth for days.

"Honey, I'm not sure that Club is *anyone* embodied," Zach said. "Except maybe Bri."

"I thought that being in the Club gave me power, but it didn't," Ania reflected. "It didn't give me power because it wasn't me. And I don't need anyone else to give me power, Anzaldua helped me realize that. I'm the one who gives me power. And I'm the one who has to decide, on my own terms, who has power over me and who doesn't."

"So, you ready to call your family then?" Zach challenged.

"I don't know if I'm ready to forgive them," she responded. "But I know that I won't let them define me anymore. And I won't let anyone shame me for not been Mexican *or* American enough. I'm ready to tell them about what I went through: the shelter, the Club, everything. I am me. I am enough."

As they left the classroom, Ania pulled out her phone. She leaned against a "Girl Power" poster in the hallway and chewed on her lower lip as she put the phone to her ear. Zach held her other hand supportively.

"*Mami?*" I heard Ania say into the phone. Her eyes darted around the hallway, her hands shook.

"It's me, Ni Ni," she said. "I miss you and I want to come home."

18 THE BIG REVEAL

My regular morning routine involved confronting my e-mail (email?) inbox that usually flooded overnight. I worked my way through each note during the day, beating back the tide, but each night after I felt like I made good progress, the troughs refilled.

That morning, a particular email caught my eye due to the curious subject line: "E Pluribus Unum," it read. Who was emailing me the motto of the United States? Was this about the free speech debate that folks had been having on campus or was it something else? And, moreover, was this something I even wanted to open? I navigated my mouse to figure out who the sender was.

D. Ho. I smiled as I saw the familiar last name. It was my former student, Dani. I clicked on the note with excitement.

Dear Prof. M,

Forgive me, but I had to write. I know how busy you are, but I wanted to tell you first. I got in. You're looking at UC Berkeley's newest PhD candidate in Rhetoric and Composition! Can you believe it? Thank you for your help and all the letters you wrote.

I have another big bit of news but would rather tell you in person- or I guess by phone. Can you call me when you get this? Same New York number.

Xoxo

D

Ps....did I get you with the subject line? It's a follow up to our last conversation about re-appropriating and making things ours. When I got in to Cal I felt like I was complete. And I felt like out of my many identities emerged one: scholar. There are so many "mes," just like there are so many "yous." I'm so many things: Asian-American, LGBTQ-American, so many hyphens. But out of my many mes I found the authority to bring everything (or would it be everyone?) together. E Pluribus Unum. *I re-appropriate the US motto for myself. Out of my many mes comes one. I define me.*

Pps.....Call me!!!!!

There were over a hundred messages in my cue, but I couldn't open a single one. I fished out my phone and dialed Dani's number. I couldn't wait to talk to them. It had been three years since I had seen them, and I really missed Dani. They had come to be such a big part of my family's life back at Pomona, and I could hardly wait to catch up.

"Prof M?" came a familiar, but somewhat changed voice.

"Dani!" I exclaimed.

"Ah, well, actually, it's *Danielle* now," came the response. The voice was definitely different, but the familiar New York City cadence the same.

"Is it? Did you?" I choked out. After two decades of writing about sexuality, I still got tripped up on pronouns and gender and sexual identity. I wondered if Dani—now Danielle—had undergone sex change surgery and processes or if this was a gender identity change. But then I looked at my email. *E Pluribus Unum:* out of the many identities, Dani was still the same person. And they would define themselves on their own terms. I didn't have the authority to do that.

"Yes and yes!" Danielle responded. "I did it, I finally did it! I started the hormone therapy and I'm on a waitlist for surgery in a few months. With any luck, I'll start at Berkeley as a full woman!"

"Wow! That is great! Congratulations!" I said. I was thrilled for Danielle. I knew how difficult the journey had been and I was so glad that she had taken this step.

"There is so much—I don't know where to start!" Danielle was breathless. I could hear her excitement through the phone.

"I mean, obviously my pronouns are 'she/her/hers' now, and I love it. And I guess, I guess I finally feel free," she added. "But, it wasn't without its bumps."

"I can only imagine," I said.

She then began telling me about a few defining experiences that had shaped the transitioning process for her. The first was her visit to a clinic to freeze her sperm before starting the hormones.

"I know I want to have kids someday, and I know it will be messy, but I felt like I had to do this," Danielle explained.

"But when I got to the clinic, they were horrible to me. Like, sperm donors and IVF couples got the royal treatment, but me, because I was coming to freeze my sperm before transitioning, they made me use a separate entrance—the back, of course—and they were just awful to me."

That experience threw Danielle, and she had almost fallen into a deep depression. But then she found a group of Asian-Americans who were also transitioning in LA, and they started a support group.

"We started reading Parker Palmer and realized that we don't have to focus on one side or the other of the 'tragic gap.' We can be the bridge that makes the in-between beautiful, no shame in this," Danielle explained.

She was referring to a popular educator-activist-poet, who is perhaps best known for his work on courage and renewal; Palmer's theory of the "tragic gap" refers to the gap between what is and what could be. As he notes in one of his pieces, "By the tragic gap I mean the gap between the hard realities around us and what we *know* is possible—not because we wish it were so, but because we've seen it with our own eyes."

Palmer notes that people find themselves swallowed up by the in-between when they get fixated both on how bad things are, and on how good they *could* be. He emphasizes that people can derive power by becoming comfortable standing *inside* the gap, and from their ability to make new things by bridging the tragic gap.

I told Danielle that I, too, had been talking about Parker Palmer with my own leadership coach for much of the past year. And that in fact, my conversations with my coach mirrored what she was saying and experiencing.

"Living in the gap—or embracing the hyphen, as I like to refer to it—is important because there is great strength in being able to bridge, connect, and birth new things," I said.

"I feel like my body has been that bridge. And that's what has given me the strength to not let others define me, but to define myself on my terms," Danielle said. "That's the only way to be."

Danielle then told me that she had repaired things with her mother in and through her transition.

"I called her and told her that she was gaining a daughter," Danielle said. "And while at first she was mourning the loss of her son, when I told her how free I felt, and how much more I felt like 'me,' and how I felt free to embrace my ancestors *and* myself, well that seemed to really resonate with her."

Danielle told me that she had documented her experiences through the transition in a text that she was working on for a magazine. We talked for several hours about transition, transformation, and embracing the hyphen. At the end, I invited her to come to ASU to give a talk to my students who seemed to be struggling with so many of the same things that Danielle had gone through over the last several years. She agreed.

Several weeks later I found myself at the podium watching the room fill with students and faculty who had come to hear Danielle read a passage from her work. Her talk was entitled "Out of many one? Or, Bridging the Tragic Gap?" I watched as Zach, AdeChike, and Ania took their seats together at the back of the room.

"*E Pluribus Unum,* Out of Many, One," Danielle began. "As a queer, trans, Asian-American male-to-female writer, I never thought I'd be quoting American mottos or tethering myself to that which is written on the Great Seal of the United States, which hangs in this White House."

I watched AdeChike nod softly, Ania take copious notes, and Zach cradle his head in his hand.

"I struggled with feeling like I wasn't enough," Danielle continued. "Like I wasn't American enough for my boyfriends, not Chinese enough for my mother, not real enough for my friends. But then I realized that I didn't have to focus on one me or the other—but that out of my many selves could come one beautiful, powerful self."

As Danielle spoke, I felt my emotions rising and falling along with her changing voice. I saw people bite back tears, shift uncomfortably, scribble furiously. After she finished, I joined her onstage to talk about my writings on living inside the hyphen.

"It took being kicked out of my ancestral home to wrap my limbs around the hyphen," I told the room. "It's often these moments of big social transformation that lend themselves to the internal dialogue that births something new."

"The journey of the hyphenated, that could be your project," Danielle interjected.

"The journey of the hyphenated is similar to the journey of the hyphen itself," I announced. "This small grammatical mark has stood the test of time, has connected words and concepts and birthed new concepts altogether." We were still in the lecture room, some of the crowd thinned out by those who had class or appointments to get to, but a core group of about a dozen or so remained munching on the snacks we provided for every keynote address.

"So it stands to reason then," said Ania. "Every American is a hyphenated American. And every American is on a journey."

"To the hyphen and the hyphenated," I said raising a glass.

ACKNOWLEDGMENTS

This book was such an absolute joy to write because of the wonderful collaborative support of Steven Beschloss and Chris Schaberg. Steven and Chris helped bring this project to life when it was nothing more than an idea. I have never worked with such terrific editors and colleagues, and I owe a huge debt of gratitude to them both.

The team at Bloomsbury has been a dream. Haaris Naqvi and Ian Bogost have provided terrific support and guidance at every turn, and I'm grateful to the Design Team for their gorgeous cover design.

Dick Nodell has been a guiding light throughout these challenging years and I would be truly lost without him. He provided key insights for this book and I often heard his voice in my head helping me when I was stuck. Steven Marsiglia provided excellent support for the book in assisting with citations and editing, and has been a formidable assistant to me this year. Erin Runions and Riva Kantowitz provided much needed reprieve and friendship when I felt I couldn't go on.

My biggest gratitude goes to my family. I wrote this book while under quarantine during Covid-19, and my phenomenal husband, Peter Kung, was kind enough to help me carve out many quiet hours of writing amidst the chaos. My three children, Tara, Shayan and Raami were all huge supporters of the project from day one. Shayan, especially, sat with me in my makeshift home office daily asking me about different types of hyphens. By the end, he said he had learned to embrace the hyphen too.

My parents, Fereshteh and Mahmood, are a consistent source of strength and inspiration. My story is their story, and I am who I am because of them. And my brother, Paasha Mahdavi, an inspiring scholar in his own right, has provided me with love and encouragement along the way. My brother Paymohn Mahdavi, who appears throughout this book, has been on this journey with me every step of the way. He is my best friend, and I can't imagine being hyphenated without him.

Finally, to my interviewees. You know who you are even though your names have been changed. Thank you for letting me into your lives and hearts. And thank you for teaching me how to embrace the hyphen.

NOTES

Chapter 1

1 Terrence Henry, "Into the Den of Spies," *The Atlantic*, November 3, 2004 (Mark Bowden, the author of "Among the Hostage-Takers," speaks about the Iran hostage crisis of 1979 and its architects' present-day struggles with the Islamic regime).

2 To the grammarian Dionysius Thrax (2nd century BC) is attributed a catalogue of ten prosodical marks, among which are the apostrophe, the (hypo)diastole, and the hyphen. See David J. Murphy, "Hyphens in Greek manuscripts," *Greek, Roman, and Byzantine Studies* 36, no. 3 (1995): 293–314.

Chapter 2

1 J. Alan. Kemp, "The Tekhne Grammatike of Dionysius Thrax: Translated into English," *Historiographia linguistica* 13, no. 2–3 (1986): 343–63.

2 Gold Circle Films presents in association with Home Box Office and MPH Entertainment, a Playtone Picture; produced by Rita Wilson, Tom Hanks, Gary Goetzman; written by Nia

Vardalos; directed by Joel Zwick. *My Big Fat Greek Wedding.*
New York: HBO Home Video, 2003.

Chapter 3

1 Zhong Yuan Jie (中元节), also known as the Hungry Ghost
Festival, traditionally falls on the 15th day of the seventh
month of the lunar calendar. In Singapore, the festival is
observed throughout the entire seventh lunar month, which
is usually around the month of August of the Western
calendar. During this period, many Chinese worship their
ancestors and make offerings to wandering souls that roam the
earth. See Goh, Pei Ki, and Goh Pei Ki, eds. *Origins of Chinese
festivals.* Singapore: Asiapac, 1997.

Chapter 4

1 Reference for (Houston 129).

2 In the mid-fifteenth century Johann Gutenberg invented a
mechanical way of making books. This was the first example
of mass production in Europe. Before Gutenberg, every book
produced in Europe had to be copied by hand. We know for
certain about this first printed Bible from a letter of March
12, 1455. On that day Enea Silvio Piccolomini, later Pope Pius
II, reported that in Frankfurt, the year before, a marvellous
man had been promoting the Bible. Piccolomini had seen
parts of it and it had such neat lettering that one could read
it without glasses. Every copy had been sold. See the *British*

Library website for more information, https://www.bl.uk/
treasures/gutenberg/basics.html

3 *The Chicago Manual of Style. 17th ed.* (Chicago: University of Chicago Press, 2017).

Chapter 7

1 *The Progressive Party: Its Record from January to July, 1916.* Theodore Roosevelt Papers. Library of Congress Manuscript Division. See also Berkeley Political Review (admin), *The Politics of the Hyphen*, November 25, 2013.

2 Theodore Roosevelt, "Roosevelt Bars the Hyphenated," *The New York Times*, October 13, 1915. Available at https://www.nytimes.com/1915/10/13/archives/roosevelt-bars-the-hypenated-no-room-in-this-country-for-dual.html.

3 Woodrow Wilson and Mario R. Di Nunzio, *Woodrow Wilson: Essential Writings and Speeches of the Scholar-President* (New York: New York University Press, 2016).

4 *The Chicago Manual of Style. 17th ed.* (Chicago: University of Chicago Press, 2017).

5 Dorothy Eagle, ed, *The Concise Oxford Dictionary of English Literature* (London: Oxford University Press, 1970, 1954).

6 John Wayne, "The Hyphen," *America: Why I Love Her*, 1973.

Chapter 8

1 George W. Bush, *President Delivers State of the Union Address* [January 29, 2002]. Published January 29, 2002.

See the *Homeland Security Digital Library* archives for more information, available at https://www.hsdl.org/?abstract&did=474718.

Chapter 10

1 Reference for link: http://blog.nyhistory.org/it-can-hyphen-here-why-the-new-york-historical-society-includes-a-hyphen/.

2 Henry H. Curran, "Ellis Island. The Commissioner of Immigration Shows How He Is Hampered," *The New York Times*, August 4, 1924. Available at https://timesmachine.nyti mes.com/timesmachine/1924/08/04/104701314.html?pag eNumber=12.

3 Reference for link: https://www.nyhistory.org/media/what-new -york-historical-society-and-why-new-york-hyphenated.

4 Henry H. Curran, "Ellis Island. The Commissioner of Immigration Shows How He Is Hampered," *The New York Times*, August 4, 1924. Available at https://timesmachine. nytimes.

5 Leonard Whitcup, "The Hyphen-Song," 1945. Available at http://blog.nyhistory.org/it-can-hyphen-here-why-the-new-york-his torical-society-includes-a-hyphen/.

Chapter 13

1 Charles McGrath, "Death-Knell. Or Death Knell," *The New York Times,* October 7, 2007. Available at https://www.nytimes. com/2007/10/07/weekinreview/07mcgrath.html.

2 Ibid.

3 Simon Rabinovitch, "Thousands of hyphens perish as English marches on," *Reuters*, September 21, 2007. Available at https://www.reuters.com/article/us-britain-hyphen-1 /thousands-of-hyphens-perish-as-english-marches-on- idUSHAR15384620070921.

4 Ibid.

5 Ben Zimmer, "The Lowly Hyphen: Reports of Its Death Are Greatly Exaggerated," *OUPblog*, September 27, 2007. Available at https://blog.oup.com/2007/09/hyphens/.

6 Ibid.

Chapter 14

1 Members of the Revolutionary Guard insisted on calling many women "*Khawhar*" meaning sister. This is often taken as a belittling and patriarchal title.

Chapter 16

1 Reference for https://support.microsoft.com/en-us/office/keep -text-together-af94e5b8-3a5a-4cb0-9c53-dea56b43d96d.

2 Reference for https://wordribbon.tips.net/T000029_Inserting _a_Non-Breaking_Hyphen.html.

INDEX